BEVERAGES

Watermelon Lime Cooler

There is nothing like the taste of fresh watermelon to cool you off on a hot summer day. This fizzy drink makes the most of my favorite melon with the addition of a few simple ingredients. Kids and adults are going to love this sweet beverage.

1/2 cup fresh lime juice

2 tablespoons sugar

8 cups cubed watermelon

3 cups ginger ale

Lime wedges, for garnish

In a small saucepan combine the lime juice and sugar over medium heat, stirring occasionally, until the sugar is dissolved. Let cool.

Place the watermelon cubes in the bowl of a food processor or blender container, and process until smooth. This may have to be done in batches depending on the size of your processor or blender. Pour the watermelon into a mesh strainer set over a large bowl. Discard the solids in the strainer, and stir the lime syrup into the liquid watermelon in the bowl. Transfer the mixture to a 2-quart pitcher, and pour in the ginger ale right before serving. Garnish the glasses with the lime wedges, if desired.

MAKES 8 TO 10 SERVINGS.

TIP: For transporting, take the watermelon and lime mixture in a sealable pitcher so it can be shaken or stirred before adding the ginger ale.

OLD SOUTH PLANTER'S PUNCH

I first sipped this sweet and tart drink at the historic Dock Street Theatre during a trip to magnificent Charleston, South Carolina. Some Charleston natives claim that the drink originated at the antebellum Planter's Hotel as the specialty of the house. Regardless of its actual history, this drink has become a classic in the iconic Southern city, and I like to believe folks have been drinking it there for centuries.

2 cups fresh orange juice

2 cups pineapple juice

$^1/_3$ cup fresh lime juice

1 cup light rum

$^1/_4$ cup grenadine

Maraschino cherries, for garnish

Stir together the orange juice, pineapple juice, lime juice, rum, and grenadine in a 2-quart pitcher. Pour the mixture over ice, and garnish it with a cherry, if desired.

MAKES 4 TO 5 SERVINGS.

SPARKLING LEMON BERRY WATER

One thing a good host knows how to do is dress up their guests' drinks, even if it's just water. At the rehearsal dinner for my wedding, my mother-in-law had large pitchers filled with water and citrus slices. It looked so pretty and tasted very refreshing. This sparkling lemon berry water is another simple way to beautify and enhance your water pitchers at an elegant outdoor gathering.

2 liters sparkling water, chilled

2 cups frozen berries (raspberries, blackberries, or blueberries)

2 lemons, sliced in $^1/_4$-inch rounds

Combine the sparkling water, berries, and lemon slices in a 4-quart pitcher. Serve chilled.

MAKES 6 SERVINGS.

TIP: Using frozen berries keeps the water chilled without using ice cubes.

BASIL STRAWBERRY LEMONADE

My grandmother always makes fresh lemonade for the kids at family picnics and gatherings. It does take extra time to squeeze the fresh lemon juice, but using the real fruit juice makes a big difference in the final product. The addition of the strawberries and basil gives this childhood favorite a sophisticated and refreshing flavor.

5 cups water, divided

1 cup sugar

3/4 cup fresh lemon juice

1/4 cup fresh basil

1 pint strawberries, stems removed

In a small saucepan heat 1 cup of water and the sugar over medium heat, stirring occasionally until the sugar is completely dissolved. Place the sugar syrup into a blender with the lemon juice, basil, and strawberries. Blend until the strawberries break down and the basil is finely chopped. Pour the strawberry mixture into a 2-quart pitcher, and then stir in the remaining 4 cups water to dilute it. Serve the lemonade over ice.

MAKES 4 TO 6 SERVINGS.

"RAISE YOUR GLASS" RASPBERRY BEER COCKTAIL

This light cocktail just might change the minds of your friends who don't typically like beer. The raspberries and lime juice add a crisp, fruity flavor while the ginger ale sweetens and carbonates the beverage. A cool glass of this concoction is just what you need at a warm summer picnic.

1/3 cup fresh lime juice

1 cup fresh raspberries (about 6 ounces)

4 (12-ounce) light beers

4 cups ginger ale

Combine the lime juice and raspberries in a pitcher and muddle together with a wooden spoon. Slowly pour the beer and ginger ale into the pitcher so that the fizz stays at a minimum. Stir gently, and serve the drink chilled.

TIP: Keep this drink in a sealable pitcher and store it in a cooler to keep the drink cold outdoors.

MAKES 4 TO 5 SERVINGS.

PICNIC IN THE PARK

FORSYTHE PARK
SAVANNAH, GEORGIA
OCTOBER
WWW.SAVANNAH.COM

It's hard not to fall in love with the town lovingly nicknamed "The Hostess of the South." Every year, once the scorching hot summer comes to a close, Forsythe Park, nestled in the center of Savannah's historic district, is home to one of Savannah's most beloved outdoor events.

Even though you will see picnic tables filled with the usual Southern fare at Picnic in the Park, it's not uncommon to see spreads complete with candelabras and fine china laid out. Each year the event has a different theme, and picnickers are encouraged to compete in the annual picnic contest by decorating their tables with elaborate designs, dressing up in costumes, and creating a menu based on the theme. Strolling around the thirty-acre park to see the unique spreads is all part of the Picnic in the Park experience.

BOURBON-SPIKED PEACH TEA

What could be more Southern on a hot summer day than a glass of sweet iced tea combined with fresh peaches and a kick of bourbon? This is a drink that truly tastes best when enjoyed outside. You may want to double the recipe, because this one goes down smooth.

3/4 cup water

1/4 cup fresh lemon juice

1 cup sugar

2 cups peeled and sliced fresh peaches, divided (about 2 medium peaches)

1 cup bourbon

4 cups freshly brewed iced tea, unsweetened

In a saucepan over high heat combine the water, lemon juice, sugar, and 1 cup of peaches. Allow the mixture to come to a boil for 2 minutes, then remove the pan from the heat, and let the mixture cool to room temperature. Once the peach syrup has cooled, pour it into a 2-quart pitcher. Add the bourbon, the remaining 1 cup peaches, and the iced tea. Stir to combine and serve over ice.

SERVES 6.

BROWN SUGAR SWEET TEA

As every good Southerner knows, you simply cannot have a gathering, especially outdoors, without our beloved sweet tea. The key to real sweet tea is dissolving the sugar. It's an easy step, but it makes all the difference. This brown sugar version gives the tea a richness that sets it apart from the original.

8 cups cold water, divided

2 family-size tea bags

3/4 cup firmly packed brown sugar

Pour 4 cups of the water into a 2-quart saucepan, and bring to a rolling boil over high heat. Remove the pan from the heat, and add the tea bags. Steep the tea for 5 minutes or a little longer if you prefer a darker tea. Remove the bags from the pan and discard. Add the brown sugar to a heatproof pitcher, and pour in the tea, stirring until the sugar is dissolved. Stir in the remaining 4 cups cold water, and serve over ice.

MAKES 6 TO 8 SERVINGS.

ORANGE DREAM SLUSH

My friend Julie and I used to make this drink when we were kids. It's almost like drinking orange sherbet. This is one drink the kiddos and the kid in you will love!

2 cups orange juice

2 cups milk

3/4 cup sugar

1 teaspoon finely grated orange peel

1/2 teaspoon vanilla extract

4 cups ice

Place the orange juice, milk, sugar, orange peel, vanilla, and ice in a blender container. Cover and blend on high until the mixture is smooth. Serve immediately.

MAKES 4 TO 6 SERVINGS.

TIP: Add a little rum to turn this into a sweet adult drink.

Coconut Milk Punch

Traditional Louisiana milk punch gets a tasty twist with creamy coconut milk. One of my good friends describes this as "Christmas on the beach." Serve this drink over ice at an outdoor brunch, but be careful—it sure goes down smooth!

1 (14-ounce) can sweetened condensed milk

1 (14-ounce) can coconut milk

4 cups low-fat or whole milk

$^1/_2$ teaspoon coconut extract

1 $^1/_2$ cups bourbon

Toasted coconut, for garnish

Whisk together the condensed milk, coconut milk, milk, coconut extract, and bourbon. Pour into a 2-quart pitcher, and serve over ice. Sprinkle with the toasted coconut, if desired.

MAKES 6 SERVINGS.

Georgia Peach Sangria

Every summer I look forward to getting amazing fresh peaches from a local "Peach Truck." The peaches are from Georgia, and each one is everything that the fruit should be: sweet, juicy, and bursting with flavor. Find the freshest peaches you can to make this "sip of summertime" sangria.

2 cups sliced fresh peaches (about 2 medium peaches)

$^1/_4$ cup fresh orange juice

2 tablespoons sugar

1 bottle dry white wine, chilled

$^1/_2$ cup peach schnapps

1 (12-ounce) can club soda

Place the peaches, orange juice, and sugar in a large pitcher, and allow the fruit to macerate for 15 to 20 minutes. Add the wine and peach schnapps. Slowly pour in the club soda right before serving. Leave the peach slices in the sangria so they will soak up the flavors in the drink. The fruit can be eaten once the serving glass is empty.

MAKES 6 SERVINGS.

MUSIC IN THE VINES

ARRINGTON VINEYARDS
Arrington, Tennessee
April through December
www.arringtonvineyards.com

Nestled in between country mansions and picturesque horse farms, you will find the best of Nashville's "Wine Country" in Arrington, Tennessee. Breathtaking views of green rolling hills and vineyards make a beautiful backdrop for an elegant evening at Arrington Vineyards. A vineyard might not be what you would expect to find in the middle of the Volunteer State, but this establishment has become a local hotspot for many reasons. Locals can't get enough of the great wine, spectacular scenery, and live music at this picture-perfect Southern winery.

Showers and birthdays are celebrated at the vineyard with a spread of finger foods especially picked to pair with Arrington's delicious wine. Not sure which wine is best for your menu? Guests are welcome to take advantage of the complimentary wine tastings offered daily at the clubhouse.

On the weekends the whole hillside of the vineyard fills up for "Music in the Vines." Since the area is full of local talent, you're sure to hear some fantastic country tunes while sipping, nibbling, and taking in the stunning Tennessee sunset.

BLACKBERRY MINT JULEP

While the mint julep is known for being the beloved drink of the annual Kentucky Derby, it's actually been around for centuries. It's a refreshing cocktail made with fresh mint and the South's favorite liquor: bourbon. This is my modern, fruity version of the old classic.

---

¹/₂ cup sugar

¹/₂ cup water

4 sprigs fresh mint, divided

1 ¹/₃ cups blackberries (about 6 ounces)

³/₄ cup bourbon

1 liter seltzer water

In a small saucepan bring the sugar, water, and 1 sprig of the mint to a simmer over medium heat, stirring occasionally until the sugar has dissolved. Remove the pan from the heat, and let the syrup cool to room temperature.

Pour the syrup into a 2-quart pitcher. Add the blackberries and the remaining 3 sprigs mint. Muddle the berries and mint together with a wooden spoon. Stir in the bourbon, and top the pitcher off with the seltzer water just before serving. Serve over ice.

MAKES 4 SERVINGS.

Caramel Apple Spiced Cider

One of my favorite activities during the fall is building big bonfires at my parent's farm. When there is an autumn chill in the air, there is nothing like a fire and some spiced cider to warm you up. Keep this in a warm slow cooker so it's hot and ready for sippin'.

Caramel Sauce
¹/₄ cup (¹/₂ stick) butter

1 cup firmly packed brown sugar

¹/₄ cup heavy cream

¹/₄ teaspoon salt

1 teaspoon vanilla extract

Cider
1 half-gallon apple cider

¹/₂ teaspoon whole cloves

3 cinnamon sticks

For the caramel sauce, place the butter, brown sugar, cream, and salt in a medium saucepan over medium heat. Cook until the butter melts, and then bring to a boil for 1 minute, stirring constantly. Remove the mixture from the heat, and stir in the vanilla.

For the cider, pour the apple cider into a slow cooker. Add the cloves, cinnamon sticks, and caramel sauce. Cover and cook on high for 2 hours, stirring occasionally. Turn the slow cooker to the warm setting and serve.

Makes 6 to 8 servings.

SHERBET PARTY PUNCH

If you're gathering for an outdoor wedding or baby shower, you must have this sherbet punch. This fruity, crowd-pleasing drink is super easy to mix up, especially with slightly softened orange sherbet.

30 ounces pineapple juice

1 liter seltzer water

1 (12-ounce) container raspberry lemonade
  concentrate, thawed

1 quart orange sherbet, slightly softened

In a large punch bowl stir together the pineapple juice, seltzer water, and raspberry lemonade concentrate. Just before serving, add scoops of the sherbet into the mixture and gently stir to combine.

TIP: There is no need to add ice to this punch. The scoops of sherbet will keep it nice and cold.

MAKES 10 TO 12 SERVINGS.

"WAKE UP!" BLOODY MARY

If you need a not-so-sweet drink for that morning tailgate, this spicy beverage is sure to get you going. Add more hot pepper sauce as needed to really give it a kick.

4 cups vegetable juice

1 (11-ounce) can tomato juice

1 cup vodka

2 teaspoons prepared horseradish

2 teaspoons Worcestershire sauce

1 to 2 teaspoons hot pepper sauce

1 tablespoon green olive juice

Celery ribs and green olives, for garnish

In a large pitcher whisk together the vegetable juice, tomato juice, vodka, horseradish, Worcestershire sauce, hot pepper sauce, and olive juice. Serve over ice, and garnish with the celery and olives, if desired.

MAKES 4 TO 5 SERVINGS.

Grapefruit Mimosas

The combination of grapefruit and orange juices in this mimosa recipe makes for a slightly more tart sparkling beverage. It's delicious for a morning tailgate or outdoor brunch.

2 cups orange juice, chilled

1 cup grapefruit juice, chilled

1 (750 ml) bottle dry champagne, chilled

Maraschino cherries, for garnish

In a large pitcher combine the orange and grapefruit juices. Top with the champagne just before serving, and garnish the pitcher or individual glasses with the cherries, if desired.

MAKES 6 SERVINGS.

SHAKESPEARE IN CLARK PARK

PHILADELPHIA, PENNSYLVANIA
SUMMER (CHECK WEBSITE FOR DATES)
SHAKESPEAREINCLARKPARK.ORG

Formed in 2005, Shakespeare in Clark Park is a theatre company committed to presenting free, outdoor productions of Shakespeare's plays, creating a cultural event for the greater Philadelphia area.

This relatively new theater experience is set in a real park—not a theatrical venue—where a perfectly shaped, immense tree provides a set of real theatricality. The actors come down the hill into their next scene, and darkness falls just as the plot turns grim. The company has cobbled together, with borrowed footlights and a generosity of talent, a real treat for a summer evening.

Guests are encouraged to bring a picnic dinner to add to this cultural tradition and memorable evening under the stars.

"Pretty in Pink" Sparkling Punch

Normally I don't like to add ice to punch because it can dilute the flavors, but with the lemonade and orange concentrates, this drink can use a little watering down. All of my girlfriends love this punch; it must be the champagne!

2 (12-ounce) cans lemonade concentrate, thawed

1 (12-ounce) can orange juice concentrate, thawed

1 (32-ounce) bottle cranberry juice cocktail

2 (750 ml) bottles dry champagne

2 oranges, sliced into $1/4$-inch-thick rounds, unpeeled

8 cups ice

Stir the lemonade concentrate, orange juice concentrate, and cranberry juice together in a large pitcher or drink dispenser. Just before serving add the champagne, orange slices, and ice.

MAKES 18 TO 20 SERVINGS.

Granny Smith, Cucumber, and Mint Infused Water

The ingredients in this recipe may seem like an odd combination, but it is the most refreshing infused water I've ever had. I like to keep a pitcher of it in my fridge all summer long and pour myself a tall glass of it to sip on the porch after a long day.

1 Granny Smith apple, cored and seeded, thinly sliced into rounds

1/2 English cucumber, thinly sliced

4 sprigs fresh mint

1 gallon water

In a large pitcher combine the apple slices, cucumber slices, mint, and water. Refrigerate for at least 1 hour before serving.

Makes 8 to 10 servings.

Tip: You may also use a traditional cucumber in this recipe. Just be sure to remove the seeds. Slice the cucumber lengthwise, and then use a spoon to scoop out the seeds. Cut into half-moon slices.

SPICED, ICED FRUIT TEA

A little sweet, a little spicy, and everything that's nice about a glass of iced fruit tea, this crowd-pleasing drink might become your go-to drink recipe for outdoor entertaining.

---

8 cups cold water, divided

2 family-size tea bags

2 cinnamon sticks

¹/₂ cup sugar

1 cup orange juice

1 cup pineapple juice

2 tablespoons fresh lemon juice

Pour 4 cups of the water into a medium saucepan, and bring to a boil over high heat. Remove the pan from the heat, and add the tea bags and cinnamon sticks. Steep the tea for 5 minutes or a little longer if you prefer a darker tea. Add the sugar to a heatproof pitcher, and pour in the tea, stirring until the sugar is dissolved. Stir in the orange juice, pineapple juice, lemon juice, and the remaining 4 cups cold water. Serve over ice.

MAKES 6 TO 8 SERVINGS.

BREAKFAST

BACON-WRAPPED HASH BROWN BITES

Cheesy hash brown casserole is a breakfast favorite in the South, so these adorable hash brown bites are my take on the classic breakfast dish. They are crispy and bite-sized, making them just right for outdoor entertaining.

24 bacon strips

1 (30-ounce) bag frozen, shredded hash browns, thawed

1 cup freshly grated Parmesan cheese

1/2 cup sliced green onions

2 tablespoons canola oil

1 teaspoon salt

1 teaspoon ground black pepper

Preheat the oven to 400 degrees. Cook the bacon in a skillet until it is chewy and easily pliable, 2 to 3 minutes per side. Place each strip of bacon in a muffin cup, making a circle around the inside of the cup and leaving an opening for the hash browns filling two 12-cup muffin tins.

In a large bowl toss together the hash browns, Parmesan, onions, oil, salt, and pepper. Spoon the hash brown mixture into each "bacon cup," and gently press down on the hash browns with the back of the spoon. Bake the hash brown bites for 20 minutes. Serve warm or at room temperature.

MAKES 24 SERVINGS.

HAM AND SWISS CROISSANTS

*As fancy as these breakfast pastries look, you would think they took some
serious time and effort to make. However, the secret is the puff pastry—
it makes you look like a pastry pro without all of the effort.*

1 (17-ounce) box puff pastry, thawed

1/2 cup apricot jam

16 slices deli ham

8 slices Swiss cheese, cut in half

1 large egg

1 tablespoon milk

Preheat the oven to 400 degrees. Roll one sheet of the puff pastry out on a lightly floured surface until it is a 10-inch square. Cut the pastry into 4 squares, and then cut each square into halves diagonally. Place the triangles on a greased rimmed baking sheet.

Spread a small amount of the jam evenly on each triangle. Place one piece of ham on each triangle, and then top the ham slice with a half slice of the cheese. Roll each triangle, starting with the long end, to form a croissant. Repeat with the remaining pastry triangles.

Whisk together the egg and milk, and then brush the egg mixture onto the croissants. Bake for 18 to 20 minutes, or until the croissants are puffed and golden brown. Let them cool slightly before serving them warm or at room temperature.

MAKES 16 SERVINGS.

Tailgating at The Grove

UNIVERSITY OF MISSISSIPPI
Oxford, Mississippi
August through November
www.olemissfb.com

Young men in bowties, Southern belles in cocktail dresses, and sterling silver platters are all part of a typical fall Saturday at The Grove in Oxford, Mississippi. If you really want to immerse yourself in a Southern football tradition, Ole Miss "Home of the Rebels" is the place to visit for a truly legendary tailgating experience.

Of course, we all take our college football seriously in the South, but most Southerners will agree that the tailgating atmosphere at The Grove is unlike any other. The Grove is actually ten acres of the Ole Miss campus shaded by beautiful oak, elm, and magnolia trees. On the day of a home game in Oxford, twenty-five thousand fans flock to The Grove for their pregame rituals of traditional Southern cuisine and "Hotty Toddy" chants. The whole area is covered in red, white, and blue tents, many of which are adorned with white table cloths, crystal chandeliers, and lace doilies.

At any other Southern football tailgate, sporting shorts and a team T-shirt might be acceptable, but that's not so if you're headed to The Grove. Everyone dresses to the nines, from sundresses and high heels to slacks and loafers. The elegant apparel is actually a sign of respect to the game and the tradition of the school. Even if the Rebels don't come away with a victory, the fans' popular saying will keep everyone's sprits high: "We may not win the game, but we'll always win the party."

HONEY BUTTERMILK BISCUIT SANDWICHES

These buttermilk biscuit sandwiches are an early-morning tailgater's dream. A "ham and cheese" sandwich never tasted so good.

2 cups plus 2 tablespoons all-purpose flour

4 teaspoons baking powder

1/4 teaspoon baking soda

3/4 teaspoon salt

6 tablespoons cold butter, cubed

1 cup plus 2 tablespoons cold buttermilk, divided

2 tablespoons honey

1 tablespoon butter, melted

6 thick-cut slices ham, cut into halves

3 slices Cheddar cheese, cut into quarters

Preheat the oven to 400 degrees. Combine the flour, baking powder, baking soda, and salt in the bowl of a food processor. Cover and pulse until well mixed. Add the cold butter, and pulse again until pea-size crumbs form. Pour the mixture into a bowl, and make a well in the center. Add 1 cup of the buttermilk in the center, and mix with your hands until all of the loose crumbs come together. Do not overmix.

Lightly flour a clean counter, and roll the dough to 1 inch thick. Use a 2-inch round biscuit cutter or a straight-sided glass to make as many biscuits as you can in the first batch, since it will be the fluffiest. Place the biscuits on a baking sheet so that they are touching. Gather the remaining dough into a disk, and roll out again. Cut the biscuits out, and place

on the baking sheet. Brush the tops of the biscuits with the remaining 2 tablespoons buttermilk, and bake for 15 minutes, or until golden.

Mix together the honey and melted butter. As soon as the biscuits come out of the oven, brush the tops with the honey mixture. Let them cool slightly, and then split the biscuits. Place one half slice of the ham and a quarter slice of the cheese on each biscuit bottom, and then place the top half back on. Serve these biscuits warm or at room temperature.

MAKES 12 SERVINGS.

Spicy Maple Sausage Balls with Mustard Dipping Sauce

*One of the first things my husband ever made for me was his Papa Mac's cheesy sausage balls.
To this day, whenever we have these addictive, bite-size snacks, he is reminded of his grandfather.
This recipe makes quite a few, but a platter of sausage balls never lasts long in a crowd!*

SAUSAGE BALLS

1 pound spicy bulk breakfast sausage

3 cups baking mix (such as Bisquick)

2 cups freshly shredded sharp Cheddar
cheese

1/4 cup maple syrup

DIPPING SAUCE

1 cup ketchup

1/4 cup Dijon mustard

2 tablespoons brown sugar

To make the sausage balls, preheat the oven to 350 degrees. Using your hands, mix together the sausage, baking mix, cheese, and maple syrup in a large bowl. Once the ingredients are well combined, roll the mixture into 1-inch balls, and place them on a rimmed baking sheet. Bake the sausage balls for 26 to 28 minutes, until they are slightly golden.

To make the dipping sauce, mix together the ketchup, mustard, and brown sugar. Serve with the sausage balls.

MAKES 40 PIECES.

SOUTHERN BELLE BLUEBERRY-PEACH PARFAITS

These refreshing parfaits are most delicious when they are made with the summer's best blueberries and peaches. They are just adorable served in mason jars, which also come with lids for easy transporting.

GRANOLA

2 cups old-fashioned oats

1 cup chopped pecans

1/4 cup canola oil

1/4 cup brown sugar

2 tablespoons honey

1 teaspoon vanilla extract

3/4 teaspoon ground cinnamon

1/2 teaspoon salt

1/2 cup raisins (optional)

PARFAITS

1 cup blueberries

1 cup peeled and chopped peaches

1 tablespoon honey

2 cups vanilla yogurt, divided

For the granola, preheat the oven to 300 degrees. Place the oats and pecans on a rimmed baking sheet. In a small saucepan stir together the oil, brown sugar, honey, vanilla, cinnamon, and salt over medium heat. Bring to a boil, and then pour over the oats and pecans. Stir until the oats and pecans are well coated. Bake the granola for 15 minutes, stir it around, and then bake it for another 15 minutes. Allow the granola to cool, and then stir in the raisins, if desired.

For the parfaits, toss together the blueberries and peaches with the honey, and begin assembling the parfaits. Place 1/4 cup of yogurt in the bottom of a cup or jar, top with 1/4 cup of the fruit, and then 1/4 cup of the granola. Repeat the layers once more, ending with the granola. Cover and chill until you are ready to serve them.

MAKES 4 SERVINGS.

MAPLE BLUEBERRY FRENCH TOAST CASSEROLE

The fresh blueberries in this mouthwatering breakfast casserole really steal the show for a morning tailgate or brunch on the porch. The convenience of doing most of the work the night before makes it great for a busy morning.

FRENCH TOAST
Cooking spray
1 loaf French bread
1 pint blueberries (about 11 ounces)
6 large eggs
1 cup milk
1 cup half-and-half
1/4 cup maple syrup
1/4 cup firmly packed brown sugar

1 teaspoon vanilla extract
1 teaspoon ground cinnamon
1/2 teaspoon salt

TOPPING
1/4 cup (1/2 stick) butter, softened
1/2 cup firmly packed brown sugar
1/2 cup all-purpose flour
1/4 teaspoon salt

For the casserole, spray a 13 x 9-inch baking dish with cooking spray. Cut or tear the bread into 2-inch chunks, and arrange them in the dish. Sprinkle the blueberries evenly on top. In a large bowl whisk the eggs, and then whisk in the milk, half-and-half, maple syrup, brown sugar, vanilla, cinnamon, and salt. Pour over the bread and blueberries, cover, and refrigerate overnight.

When you're ready to cook the casserole, preheat the oven to 350 degrees.

For the topping, use a fork to mix together the butter, brown sugar, flour, and salt in a small bowl. Use your fingers to crumble the topping over the top of the casserole. Bake the dish, uncovered, for 40 to 45 minutes. Serve warm or at room temperature.

MAKES 8 TO 10 SERVINGS.

Breakfast Sausage Stuffed Mushrooms

These bite-size 'shrooms don't need too many ingredients because the sausage adds so much wonderful flavor. Bake before heading out to a morning tailgate, and then serve warm or at room temperature. Let me tell you, a mushroom never tasted so good!

---

2 (8-ounce) packages button mushrooms

1/2 pound bulk breakfast sausage

1 cup freshly shredded Cheddar cheese

1/4 cup sliced green onions

Use a damp paper towel to clean the mushrooms. Remove the stems ,and finely chop them. Place the caps on a large rimmed baking sheet.

Preheat the oven to 375 degrees. In a skillet cook the sausage over medium-high heat until almost fully browned, for 6 to 8 minutes. Add the mushroom stems, and continue cooking for 2 to 3 minutes. Remove the skillet from the heat, and stir in the cheese and green onions. Stuff each mushroom cap with the sausage mixture, and lightly press down the stuffing in each cap to secure. Bake for 18 to 20 minutes. To transport, place the mushrooms in a dish lined with paper towels to soak up any extra grease.

MAKES 8 TO 10 SERVINGS.

MAPLE BACON MINI CINNAMON ROLLS

Based on the title of the recipe, you should know this one is a "must try." The crescent rolls make these mini cinnamon buns ideal for prepping before an outdoor brunch or morning tailgate. So satisfy that morning sweet tooth with one or four of these babies!

Cooking spray

2 (8-ounce) cans crescent rolls

2 tablespoons butter, melted

1/2 cup firmly packed brown sugar

1 tablespoon ground cinnamon

6 slices bacon

6 ounces cream cheese, softened

1/4 cup butter, softened

2 tablespoons maple syrup

1 cup powdered sugar

Preheat the oven to 375 degrees, and spray an 8- or 9-inch square baking dish with cooking spray. Spread the rolls out onto a clean, flat surface, and separate each sheet of dough into 4 rectangles. Brush the melted butter onto the dough. Mix together the brown sugar and cinnamon. Sprinkle the sugar mixture evenly onto the dough. Roll each rectangle up, and then cut each roll into 3 sections.

Place the rolls, cut side up, in the prepared dish so that their sides are touching. Lightly press them down, and then bake for 16 to 18 minutes. Let cool slightly.

Cook the bacon in a skillet over medium-high heat until it is crisp, for 6 to 8 minutes. Remove the bacon from the skillet, and drain it on paper towels. Once the bacon has cooled, chop and set aside. Combine the cream cheese, butter, maple syrup, and powdered sugar in a large bowl, and beat with an electric or hand mixer on medium speed until smooth.

Spread the maple icing on the slightly cooled rolls. Sprinkle the bacon bits over the tops. Cover the dish with aluminum foil, and place it in an insulated bag to keep these warm on the go.

MAKES 24 SERVINGS.

SAUSAGE AND GOAT CHEESE GRITS CASSEROLE

Down-home Southern grits get a sophisticated makeover in this breakfast casserole. One of my favorite breakfast spots in Asheville, North Carolina, serves goat cheese grits with honey, which was the inspiration for this recipe.

Cooking spray

1 pound mild bulk pork sausage

1 1/2 cups quick-cooking grits

6 cups low-sodium chicken broth or water

2 tablespoons butter

1 (3-ounce) log goat cheese

1 cup freshly grated Parmesan cheese

1 tablespoon honey

3/4 teaspoon salt

1/2 teaspoon ground black pepper

1/2 cup milk

8 large eggs, beaten

Preheat the oven to 350 degrees, and spray a 13 x 9-inch baking dish with cooking spray. In a skillet brown the sausage over medium-high heat, and then drain it on paper towels.

Cook the grits in a large pot according to the package directions, substituting the chicken broth for water, if desired. Remove the pot from the heat, and stir in the butter, goat cheese, Parmesan, honey, salt, and pepper. Beat the milk and eggs together in a small bowl, and then slowly add them to the warm grits. Stir in the cooked sausage.

Pour the grits into the prepared dish, and bake for 1 hour, or until the grits are no longer jiggly in the center. Serve warm.

MAKES 10 TO 12 SERVINGS.

APPETIZERS

SPICED-UP TUNA SALAD BITES

One of my mother's go-to lunches for my brother and me growing up was tuna salad. To this day, I can't recreate that tuna salad to taste exactly like hers. I have, however, come up with my own dressed-up version of this timeless favorite. These little tuna bites are simply adorable served in phyllo shells for a bite-size snack.

2 (5-ounce) cans tuna in water, drained

1/2 cup finely chopped green bell pepper

1/2 cup finely chopped red or yellow bell pepper

1/4 cup finely chopped red onion

1/3 cup mayonnaise

1 tablespoon fresh lime juice

2 teaspoons hot pepper sauce

2 teaspoons Worcestershire sauce

1/2 teaspoon salt

1/4 teaspoon ground black pepper

30 mini phyllo shells, thawed

Freshly ground black pepper (optional)

In a medium bowl combine the tuna, peppers, and onions. In a small bowl whisk together the mayonnaise, lime juice, hot pepper sauce, Worcestershire sauce, salt, and pepper.

Add the mayonnaise mixture to the tuna mixture, and mix until all of the ingredients are coated with the dressing. Place a spoonful of the tuna salad in each phyllo shell, and sprinkle them with the freshly ground black pepper, if desired. The shells can be filled an hour in advance, but if you are traveling a long distance with these, it will be best to fill them at your destination. Keep them cool until you are ready to serve.

MAKES 12 TO 14 SERVINGS.

Roasted Garlic Black-Eyed Pea Hummus

Traditionally, this dip is made with chickpeas, but black-eyed peas also make a fabulous hummus. The creamy, sweet roasted garlic is the perfect addition to this Middle Eastern dip with a Southern twist.

1/4 cup plus 1 tablespoon extra-virgin olive oil, divided

4 cloves garlic, unpeeled

1 (15-ounce) can black-eyed peas, drained and rinsed

1/2 teaspoon salt

1/2 teaspoon ground black pepper

2 tablespoons fresh lemon juice

2 tablespoons green onions, sliced

Carrots, celery, and crackers, for serving

Preheat the oven to 400 degrees. Drizzle 1 tablespoon of the olive oil over the garlic cloves, and wrap them in aluminum foil. Place the wrapped garlic in the oven for 20 minutes. Let them cool, and then peel and place in the bowl of a food processor. Add the black-eyed peas, salt, pepper, and lemon juice. Process until all of the ingredients are finely ground.

Slowly drizzle in the remaining 1/4 cup olive oil while processing until the mixture is completely smooth. Scrape the hummus into a serving bowl. Stir in the green onions, and serve with vegetable crudités or crackers.

MAKES 8 TO 10 SERVINGS.

SAILGATING

UNIVERSITY OF WASHINGTON HUSKIES FOOTBALL
SEATTLE, WASHINGTON
FALL HOME GAMES
GOHUSKIES.COM

On any fall Saturday across the United States, you will find loyal fans tailgating before their favorite football teams take the field. But there are only a couple of cities that can claim sailgating parties. Seattle is one of them.

The occupants of Husky Harbor emerge near the University of Washington stadium's east end like some sort of tailgate flotilla. They come on charters, luxury yachts, and smaller vessels, in sailboats, motorboats, and speedboats, even boats coated in purple paint. Once docked or anchored, they tailgate with a twist before taking a short hike to watch the game.

As you would expect, you will find plenty of fresh seafood and hot coffee, but barbeque, chili, and other favorites you will find at tailgates anywhere are enjoyed as well.

Touchdown Pinwheels

Pinwheels are such a convenient appetizer since they can easily be made ahead of time. However, this is not your average ham and cheese pinwheel recipe. The sweet caramelized onions, the salty bite from the bacon, and the tang from the goat cheese will be an unexpected, pleasant surprise in these festive bites.

8 slices bacon

6 cups sliced white onion (5 to 6 medium onions)

2 teaspoons fresh thyme

1 (8-ounce) package cream cheese, softened

6 ounces goat cheese, softened

$1/2$ teaspoon salt

$1/2$ teaspoon ground black pepper

6 (10-inch) flour tortillas

In a large skillet cook the bacon over medium-high heat until it is crisp. Drain on paper towels. Leave 1 tablespoon of the bacon drippings in the skillet, reduce the heat to low, and add the onions and thyme. Cook, stirring occasionally, until the onions are golden brown, for about 45 minutes.

When the bacon is cool, finely chop it and set aside.

Combine the cream cheese and goat cheese in a large bowl. Using an electric or hand mixer on medium speed, beat until they are well combined, about 1 minute. Stir in the caramelized onions, bacon, salt, and pepper until everything is well combined. Spread the mixture evenly onto the tortillas, and roll them up tightly. Wrap each rolled tortilla in plastic wrap, and refrigerate for at least 30 minutes.

Unwrap the plastic, and cut the ends off of the rolls. Use a sharp knife to cut each roll into 1-inch sections. Serve the pinwheels immediately, or place them in a cooler until you are ready to serve them.

Makes 6 to 8 servings.

Tip: Pinwheels are easiest to cut with a very sharp knife.

Bloody Mary Shrimp Shooters

These adorable shrimp shooters pack a punch that will kick off any outdoor party just right. Guests will be able to savor a delicious shrimp appetizer soaked in this flavorful "sauce," and then enjoy the rest as a spicy Bloody Mary shot.

Boiled Shrimp

8 cups water

1 lemon, cut into halves

1 tablespoon salt

2 bay leaves

1 teaspoon garlic powder

1 teaspoon onion powder

1 pound 16–20 count raw shrimp, deveined in the shell

Bloody Mary

1 1/4 cups tomato juice

1/3 cup vodka

2 tablespoons fresh lemon juice

2 teaspoons hot pepper sauce

2 teaspoons Worcestershire sauce

2 teaspoons creamy-style horseradish

1/4 teaspoon ground black pepper

For the shrimp, pour the water into a large pot. Add the lemon, salt, bay leaves, garlic powder, and onion powder, and bring to a boil over high heat. Add the shrimp, and cook for 2 to 3 minutes. As soon as the shrimp turn pink, remove them with a slotted spoon, and place them in a bowl over ice. Discard the water and lemon halves. Once the shrimp have cooled, carefully pull off the shells, leaving the tails on.

For the Bloody Mary, whisk together the tomato juice, vodka, lemon juice, hot pepper sauce, Worcestershire sauce, horseradish, and pepper. Evenly distribute this mixture among shot glasses. Place one shrimp into each glass so that the shrimp is halfway submerged in the liquid and the tail is sticking above the rim of the glass. These should be served shortly after preparing them.

Makes 8 to 10 servings.

Tip: If you are traveling with this dish, store the Bloody Mary mix and shrimp separately in a cooler, and then assemble the dish at the venue. If you are serving these in hot weather, keep the shots on ice.

Dilled Egg Salad Bruschetta

This recipe is a prime example of taking something as simple as egg salad and turning it into an elegant dish. The fresh dill and chives add a nice fresh flavor and pop of green. Serving the salad on toasty baguette slices also creates a beautiful appetizer display.

6 large eggs

1/3 cup finely chopped celery

1/4 cup mayonnaise

1 1/2 tablespoons fresh lemon juice

1 tablespoon chopped fresh dill

2 tablespoons chopped fresh chives, divided

1 teaspoon prepared yellow mustard

1/2 teaspoon salt

1/4 teaspoon ground black pepper

1 baguette, sliced diagonally into 1 1/2-inch slices

2 tablespoons extra-virgin olive oil

Place the eggs in a large pot, and cover with water. Bring the water to a boil over high heat, and boil the eggs for 12 minutes. Immediately place the eggs in a bowl of ice water to let them cool. Peel the eggs as soon as they are cool enough to handle. Roughly chop the eggs, and place in a medium bowl. Add the celery, mayonnaise, lemon juice, dill, 1 tablespoon of the chives, mustard, salt, and pepper, and gently stir to combine. Cover and refrigerate, or place in a cooler until you are ready to assemble the bruschetta.

Preheat the oven to 375 degrees. Place the baguette slices on a large baking sheet. Drizzle the bread with olive oil, and bake for 3 to 5 minutes, until slightly crisp. Store the toasts in a ziptop plastic bag.

When you are ready to assemble the bruschetta, place a hefty spoonful of egg salad on each baguette slice, and sprinkle with the remaining 1 tablespoon chives.

MAKES 6 TO 8 SERVINGS.

Sunset Symphony

TOM LEE PARK
MEMPHIS, TENNESSEE
MAY
WWW.MEMPHISINMAY.ORG

Music and barbeque are two of the defining characteristics of Memphis, Tennessee, and the traditions of both are celebrated during the annual month-long festival known as "Memphis in May." This festival is actually divided into four main events throughout the month: the Beale Street Music Festival, the International Festival, the World Championship Barbeque Contest, and the grand finale known as the "Sunset Symphony." The finale is the oldest event of the celebration, and it takes place on the banks of the Mississippi River where families bring their coolers, blankets, and chairs for a full day of fun.

The festivities begin with music from some of most talented local performers from "the Home of the Blues." Next comes an air show featuring World War II aircraft performing aerial stunts and high-speed fly-bys. As the sun sets, the legendary Memphis Symphony Orchestra takes the stage to perform soothing classical music. The evening draws to an end as a fireworks show lights up the Memphis skyline; it's the perfect ending to a perfect day.

BLUE CHEESE—
TOMATO TARTLETS

These eye-catching, mini tomato tarts are a splendid addition to any picnic spread. What could be more delicious than buttery puff pastry topped with tangy blue cheese and a fresh tomato slice? These gourmet tartlets look fancy, but they're actually a breeze to make with the help of frozen puff pastry.

1 (17-ounce) package frozen puff pastry, thawed

3/4 cup mayonnaise

3/4 cup blue cheese crumbles

18 (1/4-inch-thick) tomato slices, seeds removed (about 3 medium tomatoes)

1 large egg

1 tablespoon water

2 tablespoons canola or extra-virgin olive oil

1/2 teaspoon salt

1/2 teaspoon ground black pepper

Preheat the oven to 375 degrees. Spread the puff pastry on a lightly floured surface, and cut each sheet into 9 squares, making 18 squares total. Place the squares on two parchment paper–lined baking sheets.

Stir together the mayonnaise and blue cheese. Spread about 1 tablespoon of the mixture on each pastry square. Place a tomato slice in the middle of each square on top of the blue cheese mixture.

In a small bowl beat together the egg and water, and brush on the pastry edges. Brush the tomatoes with oil, and sprinkle the tarts

evenly with the salt and pepper. Bake for 20 to 25 minutes, or until the edges are golden brown. Let the tarts cool before serving them.

MAKES 6 TO 8 SERVINGS.

TIP: To transport or store, allow the tarts to cool completely before storing in a sealable container.

Tailgatin' Time Texas Caviar

Black-eyed peas give this spicy salsa a hearty twist. Texas caviar, a tailgating staple, tastes even better the day after it's made. Don't forget the tortilla chips for this addictive game-day delicacy.

2 (16-ounce) cans black-eyed peas, drained and rinsed

1 ¹/₂ cups chopped red bell pepper

¹/₂ cup chopped red onion

¹/₄ cup finely chopped jalapeño pepper

2 cloves garlic, finely chopped

2 tablespoons chopped fresh basil

2 tablespoons red wine vinegar

¹/₄ cup canola or extra-virgin olive oil

1 teaspoon sugar

1 teaspoon Italian seasoning

³/₄ teaspoon salt

¹/₂ teaspoon ground black pepper

Tortilla chips, for serving

In a large bowl combine the black-eyed peas, red peppers, onions, jalapeños, garlic, and basil. Gently stir. In a small bowl whisk together the vinegar, oil, sugar, Italian seasoning, salt, and pepper.

Pour the dressing over the pea mixture, and stir to coat everything completely. Refrigerate for at least 1 hour before serving with tortilla chips.

MAKES 8 TO 10 SERVINGS.

TIP: Making this recipe the day ahead gives the dressing flavors more time to soak in.

SHARP CHEDDAR—WALNUT THUMBPRINT COOKIES

At any Southern party, there are two appetizers you are sure to see: buttery cheese straws and hot pepper jelly poured over cream cheese served with crackers. For an outdoor gathering I like to combine the two traditional dishes, which results in these addictive, savory thumbprint cookies.

---

1 cup all-purpose flour

1/4 teaspoon salt

1/2 cup (1 stick) butter, softened

1 large egg yolk

1/2 cup chopped walnuts

3/4 cup freshly shredded sharp white Cheddar cheese

1/2 cup jalapeño pepper jelly (or red pepper jelly)

Preheat the oven to 350 degrees. Combine the flour, salt, and butter in a large bowl. Using an electric mixer, beat on medium speed until well combined. Mix in the egg yolk. Add the walnuts and cheese until they are well blended. (Or place flour, salt, and butter in the bowl of a food processor. Pulse to blend. Add the egg yolk and pulse. Add the walnuts and cheese, and pulse until well blended.) Form the dough into a ball, wrap it in plastic, and refrigerate for 30 minutes.

Roll the chilled dough into 1-inch balls, and place them on a greased baking sheet. Press your thumb gently in the center to make a well in each cookie, and fill the well with 1/2 teaspoon of the jelly. Bake the cookies for 20 to 22 minutes, until they are golden brown. Let cool for 10 minutes on the baking sheet, and then transfer them to a wire rack to cool completely.

MAKES 18 TO 20 SERVINGS.

TIP: These can be made a day or two before your event and stored in an airtight container, layered with parchment or waxed paper.

"HAM AND CHEESED" DEVILED EGGS

Deviled eggs are so versatile yet so wonderfully simple. I love how you can play with whatever flavors you prefer to create your own perfect deviled egg. For this recipe I decided to go with my favorite sandwich combination: ham and cheese. The combination of sharp Cheddar and salty ham with the slightly sweet yolks is a match made in hard-boiled heaven.

12 large eggs

1/2 cup light mayonnaise

1 tablespoon plus 1 teaspoon spicy prepared mustard

2 teaspoons Worcestershire sauce

1/4 teaspoon ground black pepper

1/4 teaspoon salt

1 cup freshly shredded sharp Cheddar cheese

Cooking spray

1/2 cup diced ham

Place the eggs in a large pot and cover with water. Bring the water to a boil over high heat, and boil the eggs for 12 minutes. Immediately place the eggs in a bowl of ice water to let them cool. Once the eggs have cooled, peel and slice them into halves lengthwise. Carefully remove the yolks, and place them in a medium bowl. Place the whites on a serving tray.

Mash the yolks with a fork, and then mix in the mayonnaise, mustard, Worcestershire sauce, pepper, and salt until the mixture is smooth. Fold in the cheese. Spoon the mixture evenly into the egg white halves.

Heat a skillet over medium-high heat, and spray it with cooking spray. Place the ham in the skillet, and cook and stir until the ham is browned, for 2 to 3 minutes. Top each egg evenly with the diced ham. Keep the deviled eggs refrigerated until you are ready to serve.

MAKES 24 SERVINGS.

Caramelized Vidalia Onion and Spinach Dip

Creamy spinach dips have always been one of my weaknesses, and this is one I just can't get enough of. By adding the caramelized Vidalia onions, you get a wonderful sweetness that matches perfectly with the tangy cream cheese and savory spinach.

1 tablespoon butter

1 1/2 cups thinly sliced Vidalia onion

1 (10-ounce) box frozen spinach, thawed and squeezed dry

1 (8-ounce) package light cream cheese

1 cup low-fat or whole milk

1/2 cup freshly grated Parmesan cheese

1/4 teaspoon garlic powder

1/2 teaspoon salt

1/4 teaspoon ground black pepper

Tortilla chips, for serving

In a large skillet melt the butter over medium-low heat. Add the onions, and cook, stirring occasionally, until they are golden brown, for about 30 minutes.

Add the spinach to the skillet, and stir until the spinach wilts. Reduce the heat to low, and add the cream cheese and milk. Stir until the cream cheese melts and combines well with the spinach. Add the Parmesan, garlic powder, salt, and pepper. Stir to combine well. Remove the skillet from the heat, and spoon the dip into a large bowl. Refrigerate until ready to serve with tortilla chips.

Makes 6 to 8 servings.

Green Bay Packers Tailgating

LAMBEAU FIELD
Home Games
Green Bay, Wisconsin
Packers.com

Tailgating is a time-honored tradition at Lambeau Field. In fact, some Packers' fans believe that tailgating was invented by Packers' fans back in the 1920s. While encouraged to have a good time, tailgaters need to follow rules posted on the team's website, which include space and cleaning up and things like that.

But there aren't really any rules when it comes to the kinds of food Cheeseheads prepare and enjoy. From Brats cooked with beer and onions to everything "cheese," Packers' fans love their food as much as they love their team.

HONEY GLAZED BACON-WRAPPED SHRIMP

If you are looking for a crowd-pleasing appetizer to make on the grill, the search is over! I usually double this recipe because these bacon-wrapped shrimp disappear in a hurry.

---

10 to 12 slices bacon

1 pound large shrimp

2 tablespoons honey

1 teaspoon Dijon mustard

1/2 teaspoon chipotle chili powder or regular chili powder

In a large skillet cook the bacon over medium-high heat until it just begins to brown. It should be pliable but not crisp. Remove the bacon, and drain on paper towels. When cool enough to handle, tear or cut each piece into halves. Wrap the bacon pieces around the shrimp, and secure the bacon with toothpicks.

Heat the grill to medium heat. Mix together the honey, mustard, and chipotle chili powder. Grill the bacon-wrapped shrimp for 2 minutes on each side, and then turn off the burners or move the shrimp to indirect heat. Brush the honey glaze on each side of the shrimp, and remove them from the grill. Serve warm.

MAKES 4 SERVINGS.

CAJUN ROASTED CASHEWS

Sometimes the simplest appetizers are the tastiest. I recently went to a lunch on the patio of a club house on a golf course where bowls of roasted cashews were placed on the tables for snacking. None of us could keep our hands out of those bowls, so I would say the nuts were the perfect complement to an ice-cold drink.

12 ounces raw cashews

1/2 teaspoon salt

1/2 teaspoon chili powder

1/2 teaspoon paprika

1/4 teaspoon white pepper

1/4 teaspoon garlic powder

1/4 teaspoon onion powder

1/4 teaspoon celery seed

2 tablespoons butter, melted

Preheat the oven to 350 degrees. Place the raw cashews on a rimmed baking sheet, and roast for 5 minutes. Stir and then roast for another 5 minutes. In a medium bowl mix together the salt, chili powder, paprika, white pepper, garlic powder, onion powder, and celery seed.

Add the roasted nuts to the spice mixture, and drizzle the melted butter on top. Toss until the nuts are well coated. Let the nuts cool, and then store them in an airtight container for up to 2 weeks.

MAKES 6 TO 8 SERVINGS.

TIP: These would also make a great gift for the host of a picnic or barbecue.

Peanut Butter and Jam Fruit Dip

This dip is sure to have the kiddos getting their daily serving of fruit. The strawberry jam adds just enough sweetness to the rich cream cheese and peanut butter, while the yogurt gives the dip a slight tang.

1 (8-ounce) package cream cheese, softened

1/2 cup peanut butter

3/4 cup strawberry jam

1 (5- to 6-ounce) container vanilla yogurt

1/2 teaspoon ground cinnamon

Apple slices, for dipping

Combine the cream cheese and peanut butter in a small bowl. Using an electric or hand mixer, beat on medium speed until smooth. Mix in the jam, yogurt, and cinnamon until light and fluffy. Refrigerate the dip until you are ready to serve it with plenty of apple slices.

Tip: Squeeze some lemon juice over the apple slices to keep them from turning brown.

MAKES 8 SERVINGS.

KANSAS CITY ROYALS TAILGATING

KANSAS CITY, MISSOURI
APRIL THROUGH OCTOBER
KANSASCITY.ROYALS.MLB.COM

Maybe it has something to do with the barbeque. But whatever the reason, Royals fans in Kansas City love to eat—and eat good—before their hometown baseball team gets up to bat. With some tailgaters showing up hours in advance of the game with their grills, the air is soon filled with aromas of brisket, sausages, and even vegetables. And yes, some of those vegetables are wrapped in bacon, but that's okay.

In a city that loves sports as much as Kansas City, baseball season runs right into football season so the grills and chafing dishes don't get time much to rest. The clothes just get warmer and the games move from nighttime to daytime.

SOUTH CAROLINA BOILED PEANUTS

If you have ever taken a road trip through the South, there is no doubt you've seen numerous signs for boiled peanuts. When I was a kid, we would pass these signs on our way to the beach, and my dad usually stopped at one of these roadside vendors to pick up some. I have wonderful memories of eating this unique Southern snack by the water on summer vacations.

1 pound shell-on raw peanuts

3 tablespoons salt

2 tablespoons Old Bay seasoning

Rinse the peanuts well, place in a large pot, and cover with water. Let them soak for 30 minutes. Drain and rinse them again, and place the peanuts back into the pot. Cover completely with water, and add the salt and Old Bay. Bring to a boil over high heat, cover, and reduce the heat to low. Simmer for 4 hours, or longer if you prefer a very soft peanut. Be sure to check the water throughout the cooking and add more if needed. Drain and serve warm or at room temperature. Store leftovers in the refrigerator for up to 10 days.

MAKES 10 TO 12 SERVINGS.

SMOKY JALAPEÑO POPPERS

The combination of the goat cheese and smoked Gouda in these adorable jalapeño poppers is mouthwatering. The fact that the whole thing is also wrapped in bacon just seals the deal. How can you go wrong with this winning combo?

20 to 24 slices bacon

10 to 12 jalapeño peppers

6 ounces goat cheese

1 ½ cups freshly shredded smoked Gouda cheese

Cook the bacon in a large skillet over medium-high heat until it is pliable, for 2 to 3 minutes per side. Drain on paper towels. Cut the jalepeños into halves lengthwise, and remove the seeds and veins. If you have sensitivity to pepper oil or seeds, wear gloves when handling the jalapeños. Mix together the goat cheese and Gouda in a medium bowl. Stuff each jalapeño half with the cheese mixture.

Heat the grill to medium heat. Wrap the stuffed jalepeños with the bacon strips, securing with toothpicks. Place the jalepeños on the grill with the open face up. Close the grill, and cook for 6 to 8 minutes, until the cheese is fully melted. Serve soon after grilling.

MAKES 8 TO 10 SERVINGS.

TIP: If transporting these, go ahead and stuff the jalepeños with cheese and wrap with the bacon, and then transport in a cooler and grill onsite.

BLUEBIRD ON THE MOUNTAIN

VANDERBILT'S DYER OBSERVATORY
Nashville, TN
May through October
www.dyer.vanderbilt.edu

The Bluebird Cafe is one of Nashville's most famous venues for hosting some of the city's most talented up-and-coming musicians as well as many established songwriters. In a stroke of genius, the owners decided to have a Bluebird on the Mountain concert series on the plaza of Vanderbilt's Dyer Observatory during the summer months. The observatory is atop one of the tallest hills in Nashville, providing a gorgeous sunset backdrop to the evening concerts. The casual atmosphere paired with the extreme talent make for an authentic Nashville experience.

Each group pays by the carload and brings their own chairs and picnic spreads. But don't be fooled by the casual atmosphere. This is a swanky crowd, full of the who's who of Nashville and country music. At this venue you will find sophisticated Southern-style hors d'oeuvres and some good bottles of wine. Bluebird on the Mountain has been called one of the best music venues in Music City, which is quite a declaration. Once the wine glasses are empty and the performances are over, the Seyfert Telescope is opened for attendees to end their night with some magnificent star-gazing.

Buffalo Shrimp Dip

*Buffalo chicken dip has become almost a necessity at game-day gatherings during
football season. Instead of chicken, this recipe calls for sweet and tender shrimp.
Serve it with buttery crackers, and this new favorite will be gone in a flash.*

1 (8-ounce) package cream cheese, softened

1/2 cup ranch dressing

1/4 cup buffalo sauce

8 ounces frozen, cooked shrimp, thawed and
    chopped

1/2 cup freshly shredded Cheddar cheese

3 tablespoons sliced green onions

1/4 teaspoon salt

1/4 teaspoon ground black pepper

Crackers and celery sticks, for serving

In a medium bowl mix together the cream
cheese, ranch dressing, and buffalo sauce.
Fold in the shrimp, cheese, and green
onions. Stir in the salt and pepper, cover, and
refrigerate until chilled. Serve with crackers
and celery sticks.

MAKES 10 TO 12 SERVINGS.

Gingered Fruit Salsa

*Sweet and spicy and everything nice is what this fruity salsa is all about. The small amount of
fresh ginger won't overpower the salsa, but it will give it a hint of spice, which I absolutely love.*

2 cups finely chopped, peeled apples

2 cups chopped strawberries

1 teaspoon finely grated orange peel

1/4 cup fresh orange juice

3 tablespoons brown sugar

1 teaspoon chopped, peeled fresh ginger

3/4 teaspoon ground cinnamon

Tortilla or pita chips, for serving

Toss together the apples and strawberries with
the orange peel and juice, brown sugar, ginger,
and cinnamon in a serving bowl. Refrigerate
the salsa for at least 30 minutes before serving
it. Serve with tortilla or pita chips.

MAKES 6 TO 8 SERVINGS.

Piggy Pear Tarts

When fall is in the air, these will make a quick and tasty bite-size appetizer for any outdoor occasion.

---

2 cups peeled and diced pears (about 2 pears)

2 teaspoons fresh lemon juice

6 bacon slices, cooked and chopped

¹/₃ cup chopped dried figs

¹/₃ cup blue cheese crumbles

30 frozen phyllo cups, thawed

Preheat the oven to 350 degrees. In a medium bowl toss together the pears and lemon juice. Add the bacon, figs, and blue cheese, and stir gently to combine. Spoon this mixture into the phyllo shells and bake for 10 to 12 minutes. Allow the tarts to cool, and serve at room temperature.

MAKES 12 TO 15 SERVINGS.

FANCY FIGS

Serve these dressed-up dried figs at your next elegant outdoor gathering. They pair wonderfully with a nice glass of rosé on a warm night. This appetizer looks and tastes like a real treat, but it's as easy as pie to put together.

½ cup balsamic vinegar

16 large dried figs

3 ounces cream cheese, softened

1 tablespoon maple syrup

16 pecan halves

In a medium saucepan heat the balsamic vinegar over medium heat. Bring to a simmer, and cook until slightly reduced and syrupy, for about 5 minutes. Remove the pan from the heat, and let the vinegar cool completely.

Cut the top ¼ inch off of each fig. Using a small pairing knife, scoop out the center seeds of the figs, leaving an opening for the filling. Mix together the cream cheese and the maple syrup in a small bowl. Stuff each fig with a small amount of the cream cheese mixture and one pecan half.

Place the stuffed figs on a tray or in a large container with a lid and refrigerate. Just before serving, drizzle the figs with the reduced balsamic vinegar.

MAKES 8 SERVINGS.

Toasted Pecan Pimento Cheese Dip

You can't get much more Southern than pimento cheese and pecans. There aren't a lot of ingredients in this simple recipe, so spend a little more money to buy the highest-quality ingredients you can afford. Grating your own cheese and toasting your own pecans are small steps that elevate this dish.

$2/3$ cup pecans

4 ounces cream cheese, softened

$1/2$ cup mayonnaise

2 cups freshly shredded sharp Cheddar cheese

3 tablespoons pimentos

$1/4$ teaspoon salt

$1/4$ teaspoon ground black pepper

Crackers or celery sticks, for serving

Place the pecans in a dry skillet over medium heat. Cook, tossing them occasionally, until the pecans are toasted and fragrant, for 5 to 6 minutes. Remove the skillet from the heat, and chop the pecans. Set aside 2 tablespoons for sprinkling on the finished dip.

Place the cream cheese in a large bowl. Using an electric mixer on medium speed, beat the cream cheese until it is light and fluffy. Mix in the mayonnaise, cheese, pimentos, salt, and pepper until they are well combined. Fold in the pecans. Spoon the dip into a serving dish, cover, and refrigerate. Before serving, sprinkle the reserved pecans over the dip. Serve with crackers or celery sticks.

MAKES 6 TO 8 SERVINGS.

Down-Home Ham Salad

Ham salad: there's nothing too fancy or frilly about it, but it sure does taste good on a cracker! If you need something quick, easy, and satisfying for a gathering, look no further than this tasty ham salad.

1 (1-pound) package fully cooked diced ham

2 large hard-boiled eggs, chopped

1/2 cup mayonnaise

2 tablespoons sweet pickle relish

1 tablespoon prepared yellow mustard

1/2 teaspoon ground black pepper

Bread or crackers, for serving

Stir together the ham, eggs, mayonnaise, relish, mustard, and pepper in a medium bowl. Refrigerate the salad until you are ready to serve it on sandwiches or with crackers.

MAKES 8 TO 20 SERVINGS.

3-Ingredient Lemon Fruit Dip

This sweet and tangy fruit dip is perfect with fresh strawberries, blueberries, and melon in the summertime. The secret is the store-brought lemon curd and toasted coconut. I am not a big fan of raw coconut, but when it's toasted I could eat it by the spoonful!

1 cup sweetened coconut flakes

2 cups low-fat vanilla yogurt

1 cup prepared lemon curd

Fresh berries and melon, for serving

Preheat the oven to 300 degrees. Spread the coconut on a baking sheet, and bake for 4 minutes. Toss it, and bake it for another 4 minutes. Let cool to room temperature.

In a medium bowl whisk together the yogurt and lemon curd, breaking up any lumps. Stir 3/4 cup of the toasted coconut into the yogurt mixture. Sprinkle the remaining coconut on top of the dip. Cover and refrigerate until you are ready to serve with fresh berries and melon.

MAKES 6 TO 8 SERVINGS.

SAVORY "ANTS ON A LOG"

How about this savory version of the classic "ants on a log" snack? It's a cool, creamy appetizer with a great crunch that is especially wonderful on a hot day. These are best made the day you plan to serve them so the celery stays nice and crisp.

1 stalk celery, separated into ribs

1 (8-ounce) package cream cheese, softened

1 tablespoon fresh lemon juice

1/2 teaspoon garlic powder

1/2 teaspoon paprika

1/2 teaspoon ground black pepper

1/2 teaspoon salt

1/4 cup sunflower seeds

Cut each rib of celery into about 3-inch sections. In a medium bowl mix together the cream cheese, lemon juice, garlic powder, paprika, pepper, and salt. Stuff each section of celery with the cream cheese mixture. Sprinkle the stuffed celery with the sunflower seeds, and then refrigerate until you are ready to serve.

MAKES 6 TO 8 SERVINGS.

WATERMELON-JALAPEÑO SALSA

I first tried watermelon salsa at a local farmers' market. It was made with some ruby-red melon and homegrown jalapeños, and something about that sweet and spicy combination had me hooked. I make this every summer for a simple and unique snack.

4 cups finely chopped watermelon

1/2 cup finely chopped red onion

2 tablespoons finely chopped jalapeño pepper

1/2 teaspoon salt

2 tablespoons fresh lime juice

Tortilla chips, for serving

Combine the watermelon, onions, jalapeños, salt, and lime juice in a large bowl, and toss them together. Refrigerate the salsa for no more than 4 hours before serving it with tortilla chips.

MAKES 6 TO 8 SERVINGS.

LANDRY WINERY CONCERT SERIES

WEST MONROE, LOUISIANA
MARCH THROUGH OCTOBER
WWW.LANDRYVINEYARDS.COM

Surrounded by the gorgeous hills of West Monroe, Louisiana, you will find Landry Winery, a twenty-acre, family-owned winery and tasting room. This winery was started in 1999 by Jeff and Libby Landry along with their four sons as a labor of love. During the winery's busy season, spring through the early fall, the winery hosts a concert series in the evenings. Groups are invited to bring a picnic meal to enjoy while listening to local bands play everything from traditional Zydeco and Cajun music to classic rock.

For visitors, this is an excellent way to experience true Louisiana culture. And while there, visitors can taste Landry's wines, which complement the unique cuisine of the French Acadian heritage. Cajun boudin and jambalaya, available for purchase during concert evenings, are a few of the picnic staples at this venue that you may not find in other areas of the South. If you're part of a big group, be sure to schedule a tractor tour of the winery before the concert.

SMOKED SALMON CUCUMBER BITES

These are not only a simple and tasty appetizer, they also look beautiful on a serving platter.
Be sure to assemble them shortly before serving so that the cucumbers stay fresh and crisp.

1 (8-ounce) package cream cheese, softened

2 tablespoons heavy cream

2 tablespoons fresh lemon juice

4 ounces smoked salmon, finely chopped

2 tablespoons chopped fresh dill

2 medium English cucumbers

4 to 5 slices bacon, cooked and crumbled

Combine the cream cheese, heavy cream, and lemon juice in a large bowl. Using an electric or hand mixer on medium speed, beat the mixture until it is light and fluffy. Add the salmon and the fresh dill, and continue beating until the mixture is light pink and well combined.

Cut the cucumbers into ½-inch slices on the bias. Place a spoonful of the salmon mixture on each cucumber slice. Sprinkle the crumbled bacon on top. Refrigerate the cucumber bites until you are ready to serve them.

MAKES 6 SERVINGS.

CRAB SALAD AVOCADO BOATS

There are few things I just can't resist, and crab is definitely at the top of the list. It always feels like such a treat, and this salad is so adorable heaped into the avocado shells. This is an ideal salad for the summertime, when tomatoes and peaches are really fresh and flavorful.

4 medium Haas avocados

8 ounces lump crabmeat

1 cup peeled and chopped peaches

1 cup seeded and chopped tomatoes

1 tablespoon minced jalapeño pepper

1 tablespoon fresh lemon juice

2 teaspoons honey

$1/2$ teaspoon salt

3 tablespoons minced chives

Cut the avocados in half lengthwise, and remove the pits. Carefully scoop the flesh out of the skins, and chop the avocados. Set the skins aside. In a medium bowl gently toss the avocado, crab, peaches, tomatoes, and jalapeños. Add the lemon juice, honey, and salt, and gently stir everything together to coat the salad.

Scoop the crab salad into the avocado skins, and sprinkle with chives. Chill until you are ready to serve.

MAKES 8 SERVINGS.

Kicked-Up Kentucky Beer Cheese Spread

Some say this traditional Kentucky dip is an acquired taste, but in my opinion it usually only takes a few bites to "acquire" it.

¹/₂ cup beer

2 pounds sharp Cheddar cheese, freshly shredded

1 chipotle pepper in adobo, finely chopped

1 tablespoon finely chopped shallot

1 clove garlic, finely chopped

1 teaspoon Worcestershire sauce

1 teaspoon dry mustard

Crackers and vegetables, for serving

Pour ¹/₂ cup of the beer into a measuring cup. Let it stand for 30 minutes until it is flat.

Place the cheese in the bowl of a food processor, and pulse until the cheese breaks down. Add the chipotle peppers, shallots, garlic, Worcestershire sauce, and mustard to the cheese, and process until well mixed. Add

the flat beer while continuing to pulse the cheese mixture until the spread is smooth.

Refrigerate the dip until you are ready to serve it with crackers and vegetable crudités.

MAKES 8 TO 10 SERVINGS.

CAROLINA CUP

SPRINGDALE RACE COURSE
CAMDEN, SOUTH CAROLINA
LATE MARCH
WWW.CAROLINA-CUP.ORG

Take the back roads through the countryside of the South, and you will quickly reach the conclusion that Southerners love horses. They also adore a good horse race. One of our most popular races is the prestigious Carolina Cup, sometimes hailed as the "Derby of the South." This Steeplechase is hosted by the Springdale Race Course located in Camden, South Carolina, a town steeped in Civil War history.

Since the 1930s, folks have been making their way to the Carolina Cup, which now brings in more than seventy thousand spectators each spring. The families of some of the present-day guests have been attending the race for generations, while some of the newer converts to the event come primarily for the colorful tailgating experience.

After what always seems like a long winter, late March is a time when Southerners are itching to attend outdoor events, and the Carolina Cup is at the top of the list. Ladies, especially, are eager to get decked out in the latest spring fashions, so you're sure to see plenty of Lily Pulitzer sundresses and extravagant wide-brimmed hats under the tailgating tents at the Cup. In true Carolina fashion, you'll also notice an abundance of succulent shrimp cocktail served on "Mama's best silva," just as it should be. And then, after all of that excitement, you may even see a horse race if you're lucky.

TOFFEE—CHOCOLATE CHIP CHEESE BALL

*This is a sweet appetizer that the kids will go crazy for. My sister-in-law makes
a similar recipe for family gatherings, and we all gobble it up in no time.*

1 (8-ounce) package low-fat cream cheese,
    softened

1 (5-ounce) container vanilla Greek yogurt

1/3 cup powdered sugar

1/8 teaspoon salt

1/4 cup mini chocolate chips

3/4 cup toffee bits

Apple slices or graham cracker sticks, for
    serving

Combine the cream cheese and yogurt in a
large bowl. Using an electric mixer on medium
speed, beat until the mixture is smooth. Add
the powdered sugar and salt, and beat until
smooth. Stir in the chocolate chips.

Place the mixture on a sheet of plastic
wrap, and smooth it into a round shape with
a spatula. Wrap the ball in the plastic, and
refrigerate it for at least 1 hour.

Spread the toffee bits onto a plate. Roll

the chilled cheese ball in the toffee bits, and
press the bits into the ball until it is completely
covered. Cover and refrigerate until you are
ready to serve it with sliced apples or graham
cracker sticks.

MAKES 8 TO 10 SERVINGS.

"One's Not Enough" Muffin Bites

The title pretty much says it all: one bite is most definitely not enough. This is a ginger-spiced muffin with a creamy orange and bacon filling that is out of this world. Such an adorable and addictive treat!

MUFFINS
Cooking spray

$^1/_2$ cup firmly packed dark brown sugar

1 $^1/_2$ cups all-purpose flour

1 $^1/_2$ teaspoons baking soda

1 teaspoon ground ginger

$^1/_2$ teaspoon allspice

$^1/_4$ teaspoon salt

$^1/_2$ cup buttermilk

$^1/_4$ cup molasses

1 large egg

$^1/_4$ cup ($^1/_2$ stick) butter, melted

FILLING
6 ounces cream cheese, softened

$^1/_4$ cup orange marmalade

5 slices bacon, cooked and crumbled

Preheat the oven to 350 degrees. For the muffins, spray a mini muffin tin liberally with cooking spray. In a large bowl whisk together the brown sugar, flour, baking soda, ginger, allspice, and salt.

In a medium bowl whisk together the buttermilk, molasses, egg, and butter until smooth. Stir the buttermilk mixture into the flour mixture until just combined. Fill the muffin cups about three-fourths full, and bake for 12 to 14 minutes. Remove the muffins from the oven. Let cool slightly in the tin, and then carefully remove them.

For the filling, mix together the cream cheese, marmalade, and crumbled bacon in a medium bowl. Once the muffins have cooled completely, split each one in half horizontally. Spoon some of the cream cheese mixture onto the muffin bottoms, and put the tops back on to make mini muffin sandwiches. Refrigerate the muffin bites until you are ready to serve them.

MAKES 8 TO 10 SERVINGS.

Symphony in the Summer

RAILROAD PARK
BIRMINGHAM, ALABAMA
JUNE
WWW.ALABAMASYMPHONY.ORG

The Alabama Orchestra started back in 1921 as a group of volunteer musicians, and it has since evolved into the state's only full-time professional orchestra. Every summer the orchestra puts on a free concert series at Birmingham's Railroad Park. This stunning nineteen-acre urban green space uniquely portrays railroad history while including some interesting modern design features. For the concerts, attendees can find a spot to settle in at the all-natural amphitheater, constructed from hand-cast bricks and recycled objects dating back to when the railroad was first constructed.

For adult groups, the Friday and Saturday night concerts are a perfect way to spend a summer evening listening to classical masterpieces, while the Sunday afternoon concerts are more family-oriented with selections from *The Sound of Music* and even some dance tunes such as "Twist and Shout." Since bringing your own refreshments is encouraged, locals are sure to be nibbling on Southern classics like deviled eggs and pickled shrimp followed by a slice of Alabama Lane Cake. Folks are welcome to bring their own lawn chairs and even family pets all weekend long for some laid-back entertainment in "Birmingham's Living Room."

FARMERS' MARKET WATERMELON GAZPACHO

Typically I am not a big fan of cold soups. However, there is something about this one that I just adore. Maybe it's the cooling, thirst-quenching watermelon that makes this soup so refreshing on a hot summer day. This soup is best made with the freshest vegetables you can find.

4 cups chopped watermelon

2 pounds tomatoes, chopped

1 medium cucumber, seeded, peeled, and chopped

1 medium red bell pepper, chopped

2 medium shallots, finely chopped

1 serrano pepper, finely chopped (or any hot pepper available)

1/4 cup chopped fresh basil

2 tablespoons sherry vinegar

2 tablespoons extra-virgin olive oil

1/2 teaspoon salt

1/2 teaspoon ground black pepper

Sour cream, for serving

Place the watermelon, tomatoes, cucumber, red peppers, shallots, serrano peppers, and basil in the bowl of a food processor or blender container. Process the vegetables until the mixture has a slightly chunky consistency. Add the vinegar, oil, salt, and pepper, and blend just until they are combined. Refrigerate the soup until you are ready to serve it. Serve with dollops of sour cream.

MAKES 6 TO 8 SERVINGS.

TURKEY, APPLE, AND BRIE FINGER SANDWICHES

Dainty tea sandwiches are a picnic staple. These crowd-pleasing mini turkey sandwiches get a nice creamy texture from the Brie cheese and crunchy tartness from the Granny Smith apples.

1/4 cup Dijon mustard

2 tablespoons mayonnaise

2 tablespoons honey

16 slices bread, crusts removed

16 slices deli turkey

8 ounces Brie cheese, thinly sliced

1 Granny Smith apple, thinly sliced

Mix together the mustard, mayonnaise, and honey in a small bowl. Spread this mixture onto one side of each slice of bread. For each sandwich, place 2 slices of the turkey on a slice of bread, then 2 to 3 slices of the Brie, and then 3 to 4 apples slices. Top with another slice of bread. Lightly press the sandwich, and cut into halves. Refrigerate the sandwiches until you are ready to serve them.

MAKES 16 SERVINGS.

MUSIC ON THE LAWN

THE MARTHA WASHINGTON INN AND SPA
ABINGDON, VIRGINIA
WWW.ABINGDONMUSICEXPERIENCE.COM

Visiting Abingdon, Virginia, is almost like taking a step back in time. The town, which was named after the ancestral home of Martha Washington, is a Virginia Historic Landmark. The downtown streets are lined with nineteenth-century buildings, some even dating back to the antebellum era. In fact, one of the main attractions in Abingdon is the Martha Washington Inn, built in 1832.

Every Sunday afternoon in April, classical and jazz musicians hold free concerts on the lawn of this famous inn. Music on the Lawn is part of the Abingdon Music Experience, bringing a sense of community and togetherness to this unique downtown. Picnic baskets are sure to be full of Virginia ham sandwiches and some of those famous local peanuts for snacking. It's the perfect opportunity to enjoy the fresh spring air and wonderful music at "The Martha," as it is affectionately called by the locals.

Homemade Cracker Jacks

Could there be a better snack for an outdoor movie or show than old-fashioned cracker jacks? This homemade version is a tasty, fantastic treat for kids and adults.

10 to 12 cups popped popcorn

1 cup Spanish peanuts

1/4 cup light corn syrup

2 tablespoons molasses

1/2 cup firmly packed brown sugar

1/4 cup (1/2 stick) butter, melted

1 teaspoon vanilla extract

1/2 teaspoon salt

1/4 teaspoon baking soda

Preheat the oven to 250 degrees. Place the popcorn and peanuts in a very large bowl.

In a medium heavy saucepan stir together the corn syrup, molasses, brown sugar, and butter. Bring the mixture to a boil over medium-high heat. Cook the mixture until it reaches 250 degrees on a candy thermometer. Immediately remove the hot syrup from the heat, and stir in the vanilla, salt, and baking soda. Pour the syrup over the popcorn and peanuts, and gently toss everything together, using a wooden spoon, until well coated.

Spread the coated popcorn and peanuts onto a large baking sheet or two if needed. Place them in the oven for 40 minutes, stirring the mixture halfway through baking. Let the popcorn cool completely. Break the popcorn into pieces, and store the snack mix in an airtight container.

MAKES 6 TO 8 SERVINGS.

7-LAYER BACON DIP

*Some variation of this Tex-Mex dip has been at almost every tailgating party
I have been to. I have put my own spin on it here by adding some bacon
and pinto beans. After all, everything is better with bacon, right?*

---

1 (16-ounce) can refried beans

1 (16-ounce) can pinto beans, drained and
rinsed

4 medium Hass avocados

1 tablespoon fresh lime juice

2 medium tomatoes, chopped

1/4 teaspoon salt

1 (16-ounce) container sour cream

2 cups freshly shredded Cheddar cheese

1/2 cup sliced green onions

6 slices bacon, cooked and crumbed

Tortilla chips, for serving

Mix together the refried beans and the pintos
in a medium bowl. Evenly spread the beans
into a 13 x 9-inch dish. In a medium bowl mash
together the avocados, lime juice, tomatoes,
and salt. Spread over the beans, and then
spread the sour cream on top as evenly as
possible. Sprinkle the sour cream layer with
the cheese, green onions, and then the bacon.
Cover and refrigerate this dip until you are
ready to serve it with tortilla chips.

MAKES 12 TO 14 SERVINGS.

SUMMER GARDEN SALSA

During the summertime many of us keep a bowl on our kitchen counter filled with a hodgepodge of homegrown garden produce. This salsa is an easy way to use up some of those veggies while perfectly showcasing their fresh flavors.

2 pounds tomatoes, chopped

1 medium green bell pepper, seeded and chopped

3 green onions, sliced

1 medium jalapeño pepper, seeded and finely chopped

1 clove garlic, finely chopped

1/4 cup chopped fresh cilantro

Juice of 1 medium lime

1/4 teaspoon salt

Tortilla chips, for serving

Combine the tomatoes, green peppers, green onions, jalapeños, garlic, and cilantro in a medium bowl. Add the lime juice and salt to the mixture, and toss everything together. Cover and refrigerate the salsa until you are ready to serve it with tortilla chips.

MAKES 8 TO 10 SERVINGS.

Mini Corn Dog Bites

What kid doesn't love corn dogs? They are usually reserved for fairs and festivals, but not anymore! These baked, bite-size corn dogs are quick to make, and they are sure to please a hungry crowd of kiddos.

Cooking spray

1 (8 ¹/₂-ounce) package corn muffin mix

1 large egg

¹/₃ cup whole or low-fat milk

1 teaspoon smoked paprika

¹/₂ teaspoon ground mustard

Half of 1 (14-ounce) package smoked sausage links (such as Lil' Smokies), cut into halves

Mustard and ketchup, for dipping

Preheat the oven to 400 degrees, and spray a mini muffin tin with cooking spray. Mix together the muffin mix, eggs, milk, paprika, and mustard in a medium bowl. Fill the muffin cups two-thirds full with the batter. Place a sausage half in the center of each cup, cut side up. Bake for 10 minutes. Let cool slightly before removing the bites from the tins. Serve warm.

Makes 24 servings.

Tip: Be sure not to overfill the mini muffin tins. The cornbread will rise quite a bit in the oven.

THE SANTA FE OPERA

SANTA FE, NEW MEXICO
JULY THROUGH AUGUST
SANTAFEOPERA.ORG

Since 1957, music lovers have flocked to the beautiful northern New Mexico mountains to revel in the productions at one of the finest opera festivals in the United States in a dramatic adobe theater that blends perfectly with the high desert landscape.

Performances begin close to sunset where listeners can enjoy casts drawn from the world's most talented young singers, directors, and conductors. And for some, the chance to enjoy the breathtaking New Mexico sunsets while enjoying a picnic dinner or tailgate dining just adds to a complete evening of food and music.

PEACH PROSCIUTTO BITES

This salty and sweet fresh peach appetizer is a simple yet elegant finger food for a vineyard picnic or front porch cocktail hour. Since there aren't many ingredients in these bites, be sure to find the sweetest peaches you can.

4 ounces cream cheese, softened

1 teaspoon honey

2 teaspoons fresh lemon juice

4 medium peaches, pitted and sliced into 8 wedges

8 slices prosciutto or thinly sliced ham

In a small bowl mix together the cream cheese, honey, and lemon juice until smooth. Place a teaspoon of the mixture on one side of each peach wedge. Tear or cut each prosciutto slice into 3 long strips. Wrap each peach wedge with a strip of the prosciutto. The cream cheese will help the meat stick to the peaches, but toothpicks may be used for serving. Serve immediately, or refrigerate until you are ready to serve.

MAKES 10 TO 12 SERVINGS.

SOUTHERN PICNIC
CHEESE PLATE

Cheese plates are the perfect way to get a party started. Everyone can discuss their favorites while enjoying a glass of wine. Be sure to bring the cheeses out of the cooler or refrigerator thirty minutes ahead of time to get the most flavor out of them.

8 ounces aged Cheddar cheese

8 ounces Brie cheese

8 ounces Gorgonzola cheese

1/2 cup peach preserves

1 cup whole pecans

1 pound red grapes

Crackers or toasts, for serving

Arrange the cheeses on a platter. Place the preserves in a small cup and the pecans in a separate bowl. Then arrange the grapes and crackers on the platter with the cheeses.

MAKES 12 SERVINGS.

Ham and Cheese Skewers

This is a super quick, colorful, no-fuss appetizer that everyone will enjoy snacking on.
You can replace the ham with thinly sliced turkey or roast beef if you prefer.

6 thin slices ham

1 cup cherry tomatoes

1 cup Cheddar cheese cubes

18 to 20 small sweet pickles

18 to 20 long toothpicks, for serving

Tightly roll each slice of ham up lengthwise. Cut the ham rolls into thirds or quarters, depending on how big the slices are. Skewer a tomato onto each toothpick, followed by a section of the rolled-up ham, a cheese cube, and then a sweet pickle. Repeat until all of the toothpicks are filled. Refrigerate the finished skewers until you are ready to serve them.

MAKES 18 TO 20 SERVINGS.

BLUE CHEESE, BACON, AND PLUM FLATBREAD

This flatbread has it all: a little sweet, a little savory, and a nice crunch. Naan is an Indian flatbread that is easy to find in most regular grocery stores, but any variety of flatbread will work in this recipe. The prepared flatbread can be easily sliced and packed away for a picnic since it is delicious warm or at room temperature.

4 slices bacon

1/2 cup sliced red onion

2 (3-ounce) pieces naan (flatbread)

2 tablespoons extra-virgin olive oil, divided

2 medium plums, thinly sliced

3 ounces crumbled blue cheese

1/2 cup arugula, packed

Freshly ground black pepper

Cook the bacon in a skillet over medium-high heat until slightly crisp. Drain on paper towels, and then crumble it. Reserve 1 tablespoon of the bacon drippings in the skillet. Heat the drippings over medium heat. Add the onions to the skillet, and cook until they have softened, for 8 to 10 minutes.

Preheat the oven to 400 degrees. Drizzle the naan with 1 tablespoon of the oil. Evenly top the naan with the plum slices, blue cheese, bacon crumbles, and arugula.

Drizzle the tops of the flatbreads with the remaining 1 tablespoon oil, and sprinkle with the pepper. Place the flatbreads on a baking sheet, and bake them for 12 to 15 minutes, until they are crisp. Remove them from the oven, slice as desired, and serve warm or at room temperature.

MAKES 4 SERVINGS.

PECAN-CRUSTED GOAT CHEESE SQUARES

These may look like dessert squares, but they are actually tangy, only slightly sweet hors d'oeuvres. The toasted pecan crust and tart goat cheese filling make for an irresistible bite-size snack.

Cooking spray

2 cups pecans

1/4 cup (1/2 stick) butter, melted

2 tablespoons brown sugar

1 teaspoon salt, divided

1 (8-ounce) package cream cheese, softened

4 ounces goat cheese

1 tablespoon honey

Preheat the oven to 350 degrees. Spray a 9-inch square baking dish with cooking spray. Place the pecans in the bowl of a food processor, and pulse until they are finely crushed. Add the butter, brown sugar, and 1/2 teaspoon of the salt, and continue pulsing until all of the ingredients come together. Press the pecan mixture into the dish firmly, using the bottom of a glass if needed. Bake the crust for 10 to 12 minutes, and then let it cool completely.

In a small bowl combine the cream cheese, goat cheese, honey, and the remaining 1/2 teaspoon salt. Using an electric mixer on medium speed, beat the mixture until smooth. Scrape the cream cheese mixture into the crust, and bake for 12 to 14 minutes, until the filling is set. Place on a wire rack, and let cool completely before cutting into 25 small squares. Refrigerate the squares until you are ready to serve them.

MAKES 12 TO 14 SERVINGS.

BREADS

"CAN'T BEAT IT" BACON BUTTERMILK CORNBREAD

Buttermilk is sort of a magical ingredient in baking. It has a tendency to make baked goods rich and moist. And this cornbread is no exception—it's seriously decadent. Pairing the bacon and Cheddar with the maple butter makes this recipe hard to beat.

CORNBREAD

6 slices bacon

1 cup all-purpose flour

1 cup yellow cornmeal

1/4 cup sugar

1 teaspoon baking powder

1/2 teaspoon baking soda

1/2 teaspoon salt

2 large eggs

1 cup buttermilk

1/4 cup (1/2 stick) butter, melted

3/4 cup freshly shredded Cheddar cheese

MAPLE BUTTER

1/4 cup (1/2 stick) butter, softened

1/4 cup maple syrup

For the cornbread, preheat the oven to 400 degrees. Cook the bacon in a skillet over medium-high heat until it is crisp. Drain on paper towels. When it's cool enough to handle, crumble the bacon. Reserve 1 tablespoon of the drippings, and use it to grease an 8-inch square baking dish.

In a large bowl whisk together the flour, cornmeal, sugar, baking powder, baking soda, and salt. Whisk together the eggs, buttermilk, and butter in a small bowl. Add the buttermilk mixture to the cornmeal mixture, stirring until just combined. Fold in the crumbled bacon and cheese, and pour the batter into the baking dish. Bake for 25 to 30 minutes, until a wooden pick inserted near the center comes out clean.

For the maple butter, in a small bowl mix together the butter and maple syrup until well combined. Serve with the baked cornbread.

MAKES 12 SERVINGS.

GRANDMOTHER TUCKER'S YEAST ROLLS

For part of my childhood I was fortunate to spend time with some of my great-grandmothers. One of my most vivid memories of being at my Great-Grandmother Tucker's house was the smell of these rolls baking. Thankfully, my aunt kept the recipe, and each time I make these I am reminded of those sweet memories.

1 cup warm water

1/4 cup sugar

1 (1/4-ounce) package active dry yeast

1/4 cup solid vegetable shortening

1 large egg, lightly beaten

1 teaspoon salt

3 1/2 cups all-purpose flour

2 teaspoons canola oil

2 tablespoons melted butter

Pour the water into a large bowl, and stir in the sugar and yeast. Let the mixture stand for 5 minutes, until slightly foamy or bubbly.

Add the shortening and beaten egg, and stir until well combined. Add the salt and the flour, a little at a time, stirring until smooth. (Or use an electric mixer with dough hooks to combine the ingredients.)

Grease a large bowl with the canola oil. Place the dough in the bowl, and turn it once to coat the top of the dough. Cover the bowl with a kitchen towel, and let the dough rise until doubled in size, about 2 hours.

Grease two muffin tins. Pinch off 1-inch balls of dough, and place 3 in each muffin cup. Cover with a kitchen towel again, and let rise until doubled in size, 2 to 3 hours.

Preheat the oven to 400 degrees. Brush the melted butter over the tops of the rolls. Bake for 10 to 12 minutes, until golden.

MAKES 16 TO 18 SERVINGS.

Hot Grilled Cheesy Ranch Bread

What can I say about this mouthwatering cheesy bread recipe? Butter, cheese, and ranch dressing—these are the things that dreams are made of.

¹/₄ cup ranch dressing

¹/₂ cup (1 stick) butter, softened

1 cup freshly shredded Cheddar cheese

¹/₄ cup sliced green onions

1 loaf ciabatta bread, sliced into halves lengthwise

Heat one side of a grill to medium-high heat. Mix together the ranch dressing, butter, cheese, and green onions. Spread the mixture evenly onto the open-faced ciabatta halves. Place the bread, crust side down, over indirect heat on the grill, and close the lid. Let the bread grill for 10 minutes, or until the cheese has melted and the bread is hot. Remove the bread from the grill, and slice it into "breadsticks." Serve warm.

Makes 8 to 10 servings.

Honeyed Corn Muffins

Corn muffins are sort of a staple for meals starring barbecue. These muffins are nice and sweet from the honey, and perfect for sopping up leftover juices on a plate.

Cooking spray

1 cup yellow cornmeal

1 cup all-purpose flour

1 teaspoon baking powder

1/2 teaspoon salt

1 cup whole or 2 percent milk

2 large eggs

1/4 cup (1/2 stick) butter, melted

1/4 cup sugar

1/4 cup honey

Preheat the oven to 400 degrees. Spray a 12-cup muffin tin with cooking spray. In a large bowl whisk together the cornmeal, flour, baking powder, and salt.

In a medium bowl whisk together the milk, eggs, butter, sugar, and honey. Add the milk mixture to the cornmeal mixture, and stir until just combined. Spoon the batter into the muffin cups, and bake for 16 to 18 minutes, until golden brown and firm.

MAKES 12 SERVINGS.

LEMON-GLAZED LEMON POPPY SEED BREAD

Lemon poppy seed bread has a special place in my heart. It reminds me of going to my Gran's house for the weekend. She would always make it for me to have for breakfast or to snack on while I was there. Take it to an outdoor brunch or picnic.

2 cups all-purpose flour

3/4 cup white sugar

1/2 teaspoon salt

1 1/2 teaspoons baking powder

1/4 teaspoon baking soda

2 tablespoons poppy seeds

1/2 cup (1 stick) butter, melted

1 cup vanilla yogurt

2 large eggs

1 tablespoon finely grated lemon peel

3 tablespoons fresh lemon juice, divided

1/4 cup powdered sugar

Preheat the oven to 375 degrees. Grease an 8 1/2 x 4 1/2-inch loaf pan. In a large bowl whisk together the flour, sugar, salt, baking powder, baking soda, and poppy seeds. In a medium bowl mix together the butter, yogurt, eggs, lemon peel, and 2 tablespoons of the lemon juice. Stir the yogurt mixture into the flour mixture until they are just combined. Pour the batter into the pan. Bake the bread for 45 to 55 minutes, until a wooden pick inserted near the center comes out clean. Let the bread cool in the pan for 10 minutes, remove it from the pan, and let it cool completely on a wire rack.

Mix together the remaining 1 tablespoon lemon juice and powdered sugar in a small bowl until the glaze is smooth. Evenly drizzle the glaze over the cooled bread. Slice the bread when you are ready to serve it.

MAKES 10 TO 12 SERVINGS.

Garlic Herb Drop Biscuits

Quick biscuits? No problem! The herbs in these drop biscuits give them great color and flavor. All you need is a little butter to go along with them.

2 cups all-purpose flour

1 tablespoon baking powder

1 teaspoon salt

1/2 teaspoon garlic powder

1 tablespoon finely chopped chives

1 tablespoon finely chopped dill

6 tablespoons cold butter, cut into cubes

1 cup low-fat or whole milk

Preheat the oven to 425 degrees. Place the flour, baking powder, salt, garlic powder, chives, and dill in the bowl of a food processor, and pulse until well mixed. Add the cold butter, and pulse until the mixture resembles small peas. Slowly add the milk while pulsing the dough, stopping as soon as the milk is incorporated.

Drop the dough by heaping tablespoonsful onto a baking sheet, and bake the biscuits for 12 to 14 minutes, until the tops are golden.

MAKES 14 SERVINGS.

BUCK'S BEACH BLAST

WHALEHEAD CLUB
COROLLA, NORTH CAROLINA
MAY
WWW.VISITWHALEHEAD.COM

Located along the northern Outer Banks of North Carolina is the quaint village of Corolla, a small town rich in history and culture. This area is filled with historic landmarks, including the grand Whalehead residence, originally built in the 1920s as a hunting and fishing lodge for wealthy visitors. The fully restored mansion is located on thirty-nine acres of beautiful waterfront property, and it is also the site of the annual beach music festival known as "Buck's Beach Blast." Locals and tourists alike soak in the culture of the Carolina Shag and "beach music" on the north lawn of Whalehead, overlooking Currituck Beach.

If you're not familiar with shagging, "the swing dance of the South," it's a type of dance that originated in the 1930s and '40s that involves quick footwork combined with upbeat rhythm and blues known as "beach music." Shagging actually began at open-air beach parties along the Carolina coast. Even if you're not much of a dancer, it's entertaining to watch at this all-day affair where picnics are welcome and grooving to the music is encouraged.

Sweet Onion Hushpuppies

If you're having a backyard fish fry, hushpuppies are a must for the menu. Grating the onion gives these hushpuppies a sweet onion flavor without overpowering them. Serve this Southern fried delicacy with the tartar sauce recipe in the Friday Night Fish Fry (page 238).

2 cups yellow cornmeal

1 cup self-rising flour

2 tablespoons sugar

1 teaspoon salt

1/4 teaspoon baking soda

1 teaspoon garlic powder

2 large eggs, beaten

1 1/2 cups buttermilk

1/2 cup grated sweet onion

1/4 cup sliced green onions

Canola oil, for frying

In a large bowl whisk together the cornmeal, flour, sugar, salt, baking soda, and garlic powder. Whisk in the eggs and buttermilk until they are just combined, and then stir in the sweet onions and green onions.

Pour 2 to 3 inches of oil into a Dutch oven or electric fryer, and heat to 375 degrees. Working in batches, drop tablespoonsful of batter into the oil, being careful not to overcrowd. Let the hushpuppies fry for about 2 minutes on each side. Once they are golden brown, drain them on paper towels. Serve warm.

MAKES 28 TO 30 SERVINGS.

SIDES

SUMMER SQUASH TART

Travel to any farmers' market in the summertime, and you will find a bounty of yellow squash. This tart has a flavorful crust made with fresh thyme, which is the perfect complement to the fresh squash and tomatoes. The goat cheese adds a tangy, unexpected burst of flavor. It is a beautiful tart, perfect for elegant outdoor entertaining.

CRUST

1 1/3 cups all-purpose flour

1 teaspoon fresh thyme

3/4 teaspoon salt

1/2 teaspoon ground black pepper

1/2 cup (1 stick) cold butter, cut into cubes

2 to 3 tablespoons ice water

FILLING

1 tablespoon butter

2 pounds summer squash, sliced in 1/4-inch rounds

1/2 cup thinly sliced yellow onion

1 clove garlic, finely chopped

3/4 teaspoon salt

1/2 teaspoon ground black pepper

1/4 cup goat cheese, softened

3 tablespoons chopped fresh basil

1 medium tomato, seeded and chopped

In the bowl of a food processor, combine the flour, thyme, salt, and pepper, and pulse to mix. Add the butter, and pulse until the mixture resembles small peas. Add the water through the chute with the motor running, and stop as soon as a ball is formed. Remove the dough, and form it into a disc. Wrap it in plastic wrap, and refrigerate for at least 30 minutes. This can be done ahead of time.

Preheat the oven to 350 degrees. In a large skillet melt the butter over medium heat. Add the squash and onions to the skillet, and cook until the squash is slightly softened, for 6 to 8 minutes. Add the garlic, salt, pepper, and goat cheese, stirring until the goat cheese

melts and coats the squash. Remove the skillet from the heat, and add the basil.

Roll out the chilled pie dough on a floured surface to about 12 inches in diameter, and place it in a 9-inch pie plate. Crimp the edges as desired. Pour the squash mixture into the piecrust, and top it with the chopped tomatoes. Bake the pie for 40 to 45 minutes, until golden brown. Allow the pie to cool for at least 20 minutes on a wire rack before slicing.

MAKES 8 SERVINGS.

CITRUS SPICED SWEET GRILLED CORN

When the corn is sweet in the summertime, I just can't get enough of it. I use it in all sorts of recipes, sweet and savory, but my favorite way to showcase corn is on the grill. My husband and I love a good char on our corn, which is what you will get by placing it directly on the grill. Try this method at your next backyard cookout.

---

¹/₄ cup (¹/₂ stick) butter, melted

2 ¹/₂ teaspoons Cajun seasoning

2 teaspoons finely grated orange peel

2 tablespoons fresh orange juice

1 tablespoon fresh lime juice

6 ears of corn, shucked

Heat the grill to medium-high heat. In a small bowl mix together the melted butter, Cajun seasoning, orange peel, orange juice, and lime juice. Brush about half of the mixture onto the shucked corn.

Place the corn directly over the heat, and grill it for 8 to 10 minutes, turning it every 2 minutes. Remove the corn from the grill, and brush with the remaining butter mixture. Serve immediately.

MAKES 6 SERVINGS.

MUSIC AND MOVIES ON THE LAWN

THE LONG CENTER
AUSTIN, TEXAS
JUNE THROUGH AUGUST
WWW.DO512.COM

The capital city of Texas has become a magnet for art-loving tourists who appreciate the city's array of live music venues and unique eats. Like several other Southern towns, downtown Austin hosts "movies in the park." Held on the lawn of the Long Center, the events are free. Some of the most popular movies of all time are shown on the Alamo Drafthouse's giant inflatable screen, but that's not all. Austin has added another unique element to this family-friendly event. Before the feature film begins, a local band performs a special musical tribute to the movie that is being shown.

Whether you are visiting the city or you're from around these parts, this movie event is a perfect way to end a Texas summer day. Guests are invited to find a cozy spot on the lawn, bring a picnic dinner, and then spend the evening singing along to live music and quoting lines from some of America's favorite films. All of this, with the backdrop of the sun setting over the Austin skyline, is sure to be a night to remember.

ROASTED VEGETABLE PASTA SALAD

This colorful pasta salad gets a unique, caramelized flavor from roasting the zucchini, tomato, and sweet corn. What a wonderful way to showcase the most delicious summertime vegetables.

3 large tomatoes, cut into quarters and seeded

1 ear of corn, shucked

1 cup sliced zucchini (1/2-inch rounds)

1/4 cup plus 1 tablespoon extra-virgin olive oil, divided

3/4 teaspoon salt, divided

1/2 teaspoon ground black pepper, divided

2 tablespoons fresh lemon juice

12 ounces medium pasta shells, cooked according to package directions

1/4 cup chopped fresh basil

3 ounces crumbled blue cheese

Preheat the oven to 425 degrees. Place the tomatoes, skin side down, on a baking sheet. Cut 1 inch off of each end of the corn. Place the corn on the baking sheet with the tomatoes. Place the zucchini on a separate baking sheet. Drizzle 1 tablespoon of the oil over the tomatoes and zucchini. Then sprinkle them with 1/4 teaspoon of the salt and 1/4 teaspoon of the pepper.

Place both baking sheets in the oven, and roast for 10 minutes. Remove the zucchini and toss. Return to the oven for another 10 minutes. Remove the vegetables from the oven, and let them cool slightly.

In a large bowl whisk together the lemon juice, 1/4 cup of the oil, the remaining 1/2 teaspoon salt, and the remaining 1/4 teaspoon pepper. Cut the corn off of the cob, and add the kernels to the bowl. Roughly chop the zucchini and tomatoes, and add to the bowl. Add the cooked pasta, basil, and blue cheese to the bowl, and toss to combine. Serve at room temperature or refrigerate and serve chilled.

MAKES 6 TO 8 SERVINGS.

TIP: This pasta salad is even better the day after it's made.

Honey Minted Melon Medley

There is nothing more refreshing on a hot summer day than cool, fresh melon. A quartered watermelon and a fork is a perfectly acceptable dessert in the South on a steamy July day. This combination of melons, though, gets a few simple additions that result in a salad that's bursting with flavor.

1/2 medium watermelon

1 medium honeydew

1 medium cantaloupe

2 teaspoons finely grated lime peel

2 tablespoons fresh lime juice

2 tablespoons honey

2 tablespoons chopped fresh mint

Using a melon baller or small spoon, scoop out 2 cups of melon balls from the watermelon. Repeat with the honeydew and cantaloupe to make 2 cups of each. Place the melon balls in a large bowl. In a small bowl whisk together the lime peel, lime juice, honey, and mint.

Pour the lime mixture over the melon balls, and gently toss everything together. Refrigerate the salad until you are ready to serve it.

MAKES 8 SERVINGS.

ZESTY MARINATED GREEN BEAN SALAD

Whenever I am planning a menu for an event, I always make sure to include a green side dish—not only for the health benefits, but also to ensure a colorful and appetizing spread. Fresh green beans are a summer staple. This simple recipe can easily be made ahead for a picnic.

2 pounds green beans, trimmed

1 shallot, thinly sliced

1 tablespoon sherry vinegar

1 teaspoon Dijon mustard

2 tablespoon olive oil

1/2 teaspoon salt

1/4 teaspoon ground black pepper

Bring a large pot of water to a boil. Add the green beans, and cook for 3 to 4 minutes. The beans should still be crisp. Immediately drain the beans, and place them in a bowl of ice water. Once they have cooled, drain them again, and place them in a large bowl. Add the shallots to the bowl.

In a small bowl whisk together the vinegar, mustard, oil, salt, and pepper. Pour the vinaigrette over the green beans and shallots. Toss well to coat the vegetables in the dressing. Refrigerate the dish for at least 1 hour. Serve it chilled or at room temperature.

MAKES 6 SERVINGS.

CANDIED CORN AND ROASTED OKRA SALAD

As much as we love fried okra in the South, it is best served fresh and hot, which can be challenging for an outdoor event. This recipe calls for roasting the okra, which keeps the sliminess at bay, enhancing the natural savory flavor. The corn caramelizes during the roasting, making it a sweet complement to the savory okra.

3/4 pound okra, chopped into 1/2-inch pieces

1 1/2 cups frozen corn (2 ears fresh, if available)

1 tablespoon canola oil

1 teaspoon smoked paprika

1/2 teaspoon salt

1/4 teaspoon ground black pepper

2 teaspoons lemon juice

1 cup seeded and chopped tomato

Preheat the oven to 425 degrees. Place the okra and corn on a rimmed baking sheet, and toss with the oil, paprika, salt, and pepper. Bake the vegetables for 10 minutes, stir, and return to the oven for another 10 minutes.

Place the vegetables in a bowl, and add the lemon juice and tomato. Toss and taste for seasoning. Serve at room temperature.

MAKES 4 TO 6 SERVINGS.

Spoleto Festival

MIDDLETON PLACE

Charleston, South Carolina

June

www.spoletousa.org

Charleston, South Carolina, bustles with activity year-round. However, from the end of May through the beginning of June, Charleston is busier than ever due to the annual seventeen-day Spoleto Festival. If you are a lover of performing arts, this is a Charleston attraction you won't want to miss, with daily concerts and plays hosted at some of the city's most renowned venues.

The festival ends in style, with a huge outdoor concert at Middleton Place, a national historic landmark. The gates open for the finale around 3:00 p.m., giving visitors time to tour the sixty-five acres of grounds, known as "America's oldest landscaped gardens," as well as the house museum before settling into their lawn chairs for a picnic and concert at dusk. But the fun doesn't stop with the concert itself; following the live music is a spectacular fireworks show to conclude the evening. A fitting grand finale for such an incredible festival of the arts.

BARBECUE SWEET POTATO CHIPS

The next time you volunteer to bring the chips to a cook out, surprise everyone with these crispy, homemade barbecue sweet potato chips. They are the perfect balance of sweet, spicy, and smoky.

4 medium sweet potatoes

1 tablespoon paprika

1 teaspoon salt

1/2 teaspoon ground black pepper

1 teaspoon onion powder

1 1/2 teaspoons chili powder

1 teaspoon sugar

1/4 teaspoon cayenne pepper

Canola oil, for frying

Wash and dry the sweet potatoes. Using a mandoline or sharp knife, slice them thinly. Mix together the paprika, salt, pepper, onion powder, chili powder, sugar, and cayenne in a small bowl.

Pour the oil into a large skillet or pot to a depth of 2 inches. Heat the oil to 350 degrees. Working in batches, add the potato slices in a single layer, and fry the chips for 2 to 3 minutes on each side. Be careful not to crowd the chips. Remove from the oil, drain on paper towels, and immediately sprinkle the spice mixture on the hot chips.

MAKES 6 TO 8 SERVINGS.

TIP: These chips taste best the day they are made. To store, place the cooled chips in an airtight container or ziptop bags.

Tart and Tangy Broccoli Salad

Broccoli salad can sometimes be boring, but not this one. I love its vinegary bite. Since there isn't any mayonnaise in the recipe, this dish will hold up just fine in the heat of the day.

8 cups broccoli florets (about 4 pounds broccoli)

¹/₄ cup plus 2 tablespoons canola oil, divided

³/₄ teaspoon salt, divided

¹/₂ teaspoon ground black pepper, divided

2 tablespoons sherry vinegar

2 teaspoons sugar

¹/₂ teaspoon Dijon mustard

¹/₄ cup dried cranberries

¹/₂ cup freshly shredded Cheddar cheese

Preheat the oven to 425 degrees. Place the broccoli florets on a large rimmed baking sheet, and toss them with 2 tablespoons of the oil, ¹/₂ teaspoon of the salt, and ¹/₄ teaspoon of the pepper. Roast the broccoli for 8 minutes, toss, and then roast for another 8 minutes.

In a small bowl whisk together the sherry vinegar, sugar, mustard, the remaining ¹/₄ teaspoon salt, and the remaining ¹/₄ teaspoon pepper. Slowly whisk in the remaining ¹/₄ cup oil until the vinaigrette is emulsified.

Place the roasted broccoli in a large bowl, and add the cranberries and cheese. Pour the vinaigrette over the broccoli mixture, and toss the salad together until everything is well coated. Serve at room temperature or refrigerate and serve chilled.

MAKES 4 TO 6 SERVINGS.

BILTMORE SUMMER CONCERT SERIES

THE BILTMORE
ASHEVILLE, NORTH CAROLINA
JULY THROUGH AUGUST
WWW.BILTMORE.COM

While there are countless reasons to visit the eclectic mountain town of Asheville, North Carolina, one of the most popular is the Biltmore House built by George Vanderbilt in 1889. Exploring the spectacular gardens and viewing the stunning home and Blue Ridge Mountains from the grounds are amazing experiences.

Now imagine picnicking on the front lawn with a breathtaking view of this historic home, just like the Vanderbilt family might have done more than a century ago. The summer concert series held on the South Terrace at the Biltmore allows you to do just that. Featuring top-name acts, the concert series presents various genres of music that when combined with a great meal make a perfect Southern night. The only thing that could make this evening better would be to retreat to your sleeping quarters in the mansion itself.

Dreamy, Creamy Green Potato Salad

My husband insists that he likes this green potato salad even more than the traditional version. The vibrant green color from the fresh avocado is certainly an attention grabber, and the mouthwatering flavor will have family and friends reaching for seconds. It's a Southwestern twist on Southern potato salad and just what you need to shake things up at your next picnic.

2 1/2 pounds small red potatoes, cut into quarters

1 medium avocado, peeled and chopped

1/2 cup sour cream

2 tablespoons fresh lime juice

1/4 cup chopped fresh cilantro

1/2 teaspoon paprika

1 teaspoon salt, divided

1/2 teaspoon ground black pepper

Place the potatoes in a large saucepan, cover them with water, and bring to a boil over high heat. Boil the potatoes for 12 minutes, until they are fork-tender, and then drain them.

In a large bowl mash the avocado with a fork until it is creamy. Add the sour cream, lime juice, cilantro, paprika, 1/2 teaspoon of the salt, and pepper. Add the cooked potatoes, and stir until they are completely coated. Season with the remaining 1/2 teaspoon salt. Cover and refrigerate the salad until you are ready to serve it.

MAKES 6 SERVINGS.

BLUE PECAN COLESLAW

Cool, creamy coleslaw is a must-have at my family's cookouts. My grandfather usually makes his secret recipe, which we refer to as "Pa's Slaw." This is my twist on his vinegar-based slaw that can stand on its own as a hearty side dish, not just as a sandwich topping. Go ahead and whip this up before your next picnic. It's sure to "wow" the crowd.

1/2 head purple cabbage, thinly sliced

1/2 head green cabbage, thinly sliced

2 cups shredded carrots

1 cup dried cranberries

1 cup chopped pecans

1/2 cup red wine vinegar

1/2 cup extra-virgin olive oil

2 tablespoons sugar

1 teaspoon salt

1/2 teaspoon ground black pepper

6 ounces crumbled blue cheese

In a large bowl toss together the cabbages, carrots, cranberries, and pecans. In a small bowl whisk together the vinegar, oil, sugar, salt, and pepper. Stir in the crumbled blue cheese. Pour the dressing over the cabbage mixture. Toss to coat everything completely in the dressing. Refrigerate the slaw for at least 30 minutes before serving.

MAKES 6 TO 8 SERVINGS.

"MAC AND CHEESE" PICNIC PASTA

This recipe is what I like to call comfort food, outdoor style. It is best eaten the day it's prepared, but once everyone gets a taste of it, I don't think that will be much of a problem.

2 cups elbow macaroni

1 tablespoon cider vinegar

1 teaspoon Dijon mustard

1 cup mayonnaise

1/2 cup sliced green onions

1/2 teaspoon paprika

1/2 teaspoon salt

1/4 teaspoon ground black pepper

1 cup shredded sharp Cheddar cheese

3/4 cup chopped red bell pepper

Cook the macaroni according to the package directions, and then drain, but do not rinse. Place the pasta in a large bowl, and stir in the vinegar. Let the pasta cool for 10 to 15 minutes.

In a small bowl whisk together the mustard, mayonnaise, green onions, paprika, salt, and pepper. Pour the dressing over the cooled pasta, and stir until the macaroni is coated with the dressing. Stir in the cheese and red peppers until thoroughly combined. Refrigerate the dish until you are ready to serve.

MAKES 6 SERVINGS.

GARDEN FRESH TOMATO AND PEACH SALAD

This is a fresh and fabulous salad that is perfect for a hot summer day. I can't think of a better way to showcase the South's freshest tomatoes and peaches. It is a simple but elegant dish that could not be easier to toss together.

3 tablespoons white balsamic vinegar

1 1/2 teaspoons Dijon mustard

2 teaspoons honey

1/2 teaspoon salt

1/4 teaspoon ground black pepper

1/4 cup extra-virgin olive oil

1/4 cup fresh basil, chopped

3 medium ripe peaches, sliced into wedges

3 medium tomatoes, sliced into wedges

1/2 cup thinly sliced red onion

In a large bowl whisk together the balsamic vinegar, mustard, honey, salt, and pepper. Slowly drizzle in the olive oil, whisking constantly, and then stir in the basil.

Add the peaches, tomatoes, and onions to the bowl and toss everything together gently. This salad is best served at room temperature.

MAKES 6 TO 8 SERVINGS.

Red Wine Grilled 'Shrooms

These savory mushrooms can stand on their own or serve as a hearty topper for steaks or burgers. The splash of red wine gives these mushrooms a sophisticated flavor with very little effort.

1 (16-ounce) package baby bella mushrooms, sliced

1 cup chopped white onion

2 cloves garlic, finely chopped

1/4 cup red wine

1/2 teaspoon salt

1/2 teaspoon ground black pepper

3 tablespoons butter, sliced into pats

Heat the grill to medium heat. Place the mushrooms, onions, and garlic on a sheet of aluminum foil. You might want to place the aluminum foil in a shallow dish or bowl to keep the liquid from running out. Pour the wine over the mushrooms, and sprinkle with the salt and pepper. Top the mixture with pats of the butter. Place another sheet of aluminum foil on top, and fold the edges together to seal. Place the packet on the grill for 10 minutes, flip, and cook for another 10 minutes. Keep the packet sealed until you are ready to serve the mushrooms.

Makes 6 servings.

Tip: To travel with this, prepare the packets ahead of time so they are ready to grill on location.

BRITTFEST

JACKSONVILLE, OREGON
CONCERTS FROM SPRING THROUGH FALL
BRITTFEST.ORG

B rittfest is the Pacific Northwest's premier outdoor summer performing arts festival. Located in the historic 1850's gold rush town of Jacksonville, Oregon, Brittfest presents dozens of summer concerts featuring world-class artists in classical, jazz, blues, folk, bluegrass, world, pop, and country music.

Brittfest's performance venue is a naturally formed amphitheater set among majestic ponderosa pines and native madrones on the beautiful hillside estate of nineteenth-century photographer Peter Britt, whose remarkable life is still visible on the Britt hill. A reconstructed stone foundation outlines Peter Britt's original home site in the lower gardens. Many of the trees Britt planted are still producing fruit, and the Sequoia sapling Britt planted on the day his first child was born in 1862 now stands more than two hundred feet tall.

Tens of thousands of music lovers travel from all over the West to enjoy Brittfest's world-class performances, spectacular scenery, and casual, relaxing atmosphere. While there, they enjoy picnics brought from home as well as the festival's diverse concessions menu.

OLD-FASHIONED GREEN PEA AND HAM SALAD

Sometimes the simplest dishes are the best ones. A picnic favorite, this ham and pea salad is a traditional side dish that's a cinch to whip up. The salty ham and sweet green peas make a yummy pair.

4 cups frozen peas, thawed

1 cup small-diced ham

1/2 cup finely chopped red onion

2/3 cup mayonnaise

2 tablespoons cider vinegar

1 teaspoon sugar

1/2 teaspoon salt

1/2 teaspoon ground black pepper

In a large bowl combine the peas, ham, and onions. In a small bowl whisk together the mayonnaise, vinegar, sugar, salt, and pepper. Pour the dressing over the pea mixture, and stir until all of the ingredients are coated. Refrigerate this dish until you are ready to serve it.

MAKES 8 SERVINGS.

"End of Summer" Grilled Green Tomatoes

It almost doesn't sound right not to have the word fried in front of green tomatoes. However, this sweet and tangy glaze along with a nice char on unripe tomatoes make for an absolutely fantastic end of the season side dish or burger topper.

2 tablespoons balsamic vinegar

1 tablespoon brown sugar

2 tablespoons extra-virgin olive oil

$^1\!/_2$ teaspoon salt

$^1\!/_4$ teaspoon ground black pepper

4 large green tomatoes, cut into $^1\!/_2$-inch slices

Heat the grill to medium-high heat. Whisk together the balsamic vinegar, brown sugar, oil, salt, and pepper in a small bowl. Place the tomato slices on the grill, and brush with the vinegar mixture. Grill for 2 to 3 minutes per side, continuing to brush the vinegar mixture on the slices as they cook. Serve immediately.

MAKES 6 TO 8 SERVINGS.

GATHERING ON THE GREEN

OLD CAPITOL MUSEUM LAWN
Jackson, Mississippi
Saturday in April
WWW.GATHERINGONTHEGREEN.ORG

Jackson, Mississippi, is holding on to the tradition of hosting events on the old capitol green, which Mississippians have been doing for the past 180 years. Gathering on the Green is held on the only remaining green space on the lawn of the city's oldest building. This event promotes all that the city of Jackson has to offer in history and the arts. It's a family-friendly event where the locals can pack up their picnic baskets and enjoy a day on "the city's front yard."

The celebration begins on a Saturday morning in April, and the fun continues into the afternoon. Attendees get to experience the work of some of Jackson's finest craftsmen and even Civil War reenactments. Meanwhile, the kids stay entertained with a variety of old-fashioned games and a mini archeological dig on the lawn. In between activities, guests are welcome to spread out their picnic blankets and enjoy live Civil War–era music. Gathering on the Green is bringing this Southern town together in celebration of the rich of this "city with soul."

Poblano and Corn Chow Chow

Chow chow is a fantastic Southern condiment that goes with all things grilled or smoked. It's sweet and tangy, and we love it on most anything.

---

1 medium red bell pepper, chopped

1 poblano pepper, chopped

1 1/2 cups chopped white onion

2 cups frozen or fresh corn kernels, thawed

1/2 cup cider vinegar

1/2 cup sugar

1 1/2 teaspoons salt

1/2 teaspoon dry mustard

1/2 teaspoon ground cumin

1/2 teaspoon ground black pepper

Place the red peppers, poblano, and onions in the bowl of a food processor. Pulse until a salsa consistency is formed. Don't over mix. The ingredients should still be distinguishable from one another. Place the pepper mixture into a large saucepan, and add the corn, vinegar, sugar, salt, mustard, cumin, and pepper. Bring the mixture to a boil over medium-high heat, reduce the heat to low, and cook for another 15 minutes. Place the chow chow in an airtight container, and refrigerate it until you are ready to serve.

MAKES 10 TO 12 SERVINGS.

Heirloom Beet and Orange Salad

This beet salad has a way of changing folks' minds about beets. The beautiful colors in this dish are enough to sell most. It's sophisticated and simple, perfect for a fancy picnic.

2 pounds medium red and golden beets

4 tablespoons extra-virgin olive oil, divided

2 medium oranges, peeled and sliced into rounds

1 1/2 tablespoons white balsamic vinegar

2 teaspoons honey

1/2 teaspoon salt

1/4 teaspoon ground black pepper

1/2 cup chopped walnuts

3 ounces crumbled goat cheese

Preheat the oven to 400 degrees. Cut off the tops of the beets. Place the beets on small squares of aluminum foil, and drizzle them with 1 tablespoon of the oil. Wrap the foil around the beets securely. Place them on a baking sheet, and roast them for 1 hour. Let them cool completely. Unwrap the beets, and then peel and slice them into 1/4-inch thick rounds. Layer the beet rounds and the orange rounds in a shallow dish.

In a small bowl whisk together the balsamic vinegar, honey, salt, and pepper. Slowly drizzle in the remaining 3 tablespoons oil while whisking. Pour the vinaigrette over the beets and oranges. Top them with the walnuts and goat cheese. Serve this dish at room temperature or refrigerate and serve chilled.

MAKES 4 TO 6 SERVINGS.

Marinated Summer Squash Ribbons

With the abundance of yellow squash during the summer, I've come up with countless ways to prepare it. Now you have a new way. This is a great recipe to take to an outside event because there is no cooking involved and no temperature requirement.

4 medium summer squash

1/4 cup extra-virgin olive oil

2 tablespoons fresh lemon juice

2 teaspoons honey

1/2 teaspoon salt

1/4 teaspoon ground black pepper

1 clove garlic, finely chopped

2 tablespoons chopped fresh parsley

Using a vegetable peeler or mandoline, thinly slice the squash lengthwise. Place the slices in a large bowl. In a small bowl whisk together the oil, lemon juice, honey, salt, pepper, garlic, and parsley. Pour the dressing over the squash, and toss together gently. Refrigerate the dish for at least 30 minutes before serving it.

MAKES 4 TO 6 SERVINGS.

HAM AND WHITE BEAN CORNBREAD SALAD

Ham and white beans are one of my favorite Southern combinations so I used that concept to come up with this tasty cornbread salad. Let's just say, this salad is totally worth making a batch of cornbread for. This is a recipe everyone will be begging for!

BUTTERMILK DRESSING

1/2 cup mayonnaise

1/2 cup sour cream

1/2 cup buttermilk

2 tablespoons fresh lemon juice

1/2 teaspoon garlic powder

1/2 teaspoon onion powder

1/2 teaspoon dried dill

1/2 teaspoon ground black pepper

1/2 teaspoon salt

SALAD

1 (8 1/2-ounce) package cornbread mix, prepared and cubed

2 (15-ounce) cans white beans, drained and rinsed

2 cups chopped tomatoes

1/2 cup sliced green onions, divided

1 1/2 cups frozen corn, thawed

1 1/2 cups cubed ham

1 medium green bell pepper, chopped

1 1/2 cups freshly shredded Cheddar cheese

For the dressing, in a medium bowl whisk together the mayonnaise, sour cream, buttermilk, lemon juice, garlic powder, onion powder, dill, pepper, and salt.

For the salad, fill the bottom of a large glass bowl or trifle dish with the cornbread cubes. Layer on the remaining ingredients, starting with the beans, tomatoes, 1/4 cup of the green onions, corn, ham, green peppers, and cheese. Spread the dressing on top of the cheese, and top the salad with the remaining 1/4 cup green onions. Cover the dish with plastic wrap, and refrigerate until you are ready to serve it.

MAKES 10 TO 12 SERVINGS.

Charred Okra Skewers with Smoky Buttermilk Dipping Sauce

If you haven't tried grilling okra, I would highly recommend it. The charred flavor is a wonderful complement to this smoky buttermilk dipping sauce. Serve the okra on a big platter with the dipping sauce in the middle, similar to the way you'd serve chips and salsa.

Dipping Sauce

1/4 cup buttermilk

1/4 cup mayonnaise

1/2 teaspoon paprika

1/4 teaspoon ground cumin

1/4 teaspoon salt

Okra

2 pounds okra

2 tablespoons canola oil

2 tablespoons fresh lemon juice

3/4 teaspoon salt

1/2 teaspoon ground black pepper

For the dipping sauce, in a small bowl whisk together the buttermilk, mayonnaise, paprika, cumin, and salt. Refrigerate the sauce until you are ready to serve the okra.

For the okra, heat the grill to medium-high heat. In a large bowl toss together the okra, oil, lemon juice, salt, and pepper. Place about 6 okra pods on each skewer. Grill the okra for 4 to 5 minutes per side, until each side is charred. Serve the grilled okra with the dipping sauce.

Makes 4 to 6 servings.

Tip: To transport this dish, make the sauce and skewer the okra ahead of time, and then just grill the okra on-site.

MILLER OUTDOOR THEATRE

HERMANN PARK
HOUSTON, TEXAS
MARCH THROUGH NOVEMBER
WWW.MILLEROUTDOORTHEATRE.COM

It has become a tradition for many Houstonians: checking to see what's playing for the evening, packing a cooler, and heading over to Hermann Park for a performance at the Miller Outdoor Theatre. From musicals to movies to ballet, this seven-acre venue hosts productions as diverse as the city itself. With an eight-month season of entertainment, seating for 1,700 people, plus a lawn on the hillside with room for 4,500 picnickers, it's easy to catch a show if you're in the area. The performances are "always free" at the Miller, the largest free outdoor theatre in the country.

Not only does the theatre offer weekend performances under the stars, but it also hosts childrens' plays during the week making it the perfect, inexpensive day-time outing with the kids during summer break. Why not make a day of it by exploring Hermann Park, also home to the Houston Museum of Natural Science and the Houston Zoo, and then end the night with a relaxing picnic on the hillside of this visually stunning outdoor theatre?

"Grape Expectations" Wild Rice Pilaf

A rice dish might not be your first thought for outdoor entertaining, but this fruity wild rice pilaf actually makes an excellent side dish for an outdoor luncheon. It does not have to be kept warm or cold, and it tastes even better if it's made the day before serving.

2 1/2 cups low-sodium chicken broth or water

1 cup wild rice

1 teaspoon finely grated orange peel

2 tablespoons fresh orange juice

2 tablespoons butter, melted

1 cup red grapes, cut into halves

1/2 cup sliced almonds

1/4 cup dried cranberries

1/4 cup sliced green onions

1 teaspoon salt

1/4 teaspoon ground black pepper

Place the broth in a medium saucepan, and bring it to a boil over high heat. Add the rice, and cook according to package directions. Let the rice cool for 20 minutes. Put the rice in a medium bowl, and stir in the orange peel, orange juice, butter, grapes, almonds, cranberries, green onions, salt, and pepper.

Serve at room temperature, or refrigerate the dish until you are ready to serve it.

MAKES 6 SERVINGS.

Brown Sugar and Bacon Sweet Potato Salad

There are hundreds of potato salads out there. Here is one you may not have tried, though. It's got that sweet and savory combo going on that you will love.

Dressing

3 tablespoons cider vinegar

1 teaspoon Dijon mustard

2 teaspoons brown sugar

$1/2$ teaspoon paprika

$1/2$ teaspoon ancho chili powder

$1/4$ teaspoon salt

$1/4$ teaspoon ground black pepper

$1/3$ cup extra virgin olive oil

Salad

2 $1/2$ pounds sweet potatoes, peeled and cubed

1 cup roughly chopped red onion

2 tablespoons extra-virgin olive oil

$1/2$ teaspoon salt

4 slices bacon

For the dressing, in a small bowl whisk together the vinegar, mustard, brown sugar, paprika, chili powder, salt, and pepper. Slowly whisk in the oil until the dressing is emulsified.

For the salad, preheat the oven to 425 degrees. Place the sweet potatoes and onions on a large rimmed baking sheet, and toss with the oil and salt. Bake for 16 to 18 minutes, until the potatoes are soft. Cook the bacon in a skillet over medium-high heat until it is crisp. Drain it on paper towels, crumble it when cool enough to handle, and place in a large bowl. Add the potatoes and onions while they are still warm to the bacon. Pour in the dressing, and toss everything together until the potatoes are well coated. Serve warm or at room temperature.

Makes 6 to 8 servings.

"CLEANSE YOUR PALATE" CELERY SALAD

With all of the tasty barbecued dishes and mayonnaise-based salads in the summertime, it's nice to have a simple palate-cleansing side dish on your plate as well. This celery salad could not be easier, and it has such a refreshingly clean flavor. The crunch from the celery and apples and the sweet and chewy raisins come together to make this side dish unique.

2 cups chopped celery

1 cup chopped unpeeled apple

1/4 cup raisins

1/4 cup chopped pecans

2 tablespoons chopped fresh parsley

2 tablespoons fresh lemon juice

2 teaspoons honey

1/4 teaspoon salt

1/8 teaspoon ground black pepper

In a medium bowl toss together the celery, apples, raisins, and pecans. In a small bowl mix together the parsley, lemon juice, honey, salt, and pepper. Pour the dressing over the salad, and toss everything together. Refrigerate the salad until you are ready to serve it.

MAKES 6 TO 8 SERVINGS.

GIGI'S WHIPPED CREAM FRUIT SALAD

This delicious fruit salad is one that I had for the first time at my mother-in-law's house, who is now affectionately known as Gigi, thanks to her grandchildren. The salad is creamy and fluffy without being overly sweet, so it still works as a side dish.

2 cups chopped, peeled apples

2 cups chopped, peeled oranges

2 cups grapes, cut into halves

2 cups sliced bananas

1 1/2 cups cold heavy cream

3 tablespoons sugar

1 teaspoon finely grated orange peel

1/2 teaspoon almond extract

1/2 cup chopped walnuts

Place the apples, oranges, grapes, and bananas in a large bowl, and toss together. In a large bowl beat the cream using an electric mixer on medium speed until it begins to thicken. Slowly add the sugar while beating until soft peaks are formed. Add the orange peel and almond extract, and beat until blended.

Pour the whipped cream over the fruit, and gently fold it into the salad along with the walnuts. Refrigerate the salad until you are ready to serve it.

MAKES 8 TO 10 SERVINGS.

SOUTHWESTERN CRUSTLESS CORN QUICHE

"Quiche of the day" is a common menu item for "ladies who lunch." This quiche has a Southwestern flair from the green chilies, which are fantastic with the sweet corn and savory bacon.

3 slices bacon

$1/2$ cup chopped red onion

2 cups frozen corn kernels, thawed

5 large eggs

1 cup heavy cream

$1/2$ cup milk

1 (4-ounce) can chopped green chilies

1 $1/2$ cups shredded Mexican-style cheese

$1/2$ teaspoon salt

$1/2$ teaspoon ground black pepper

Place the bacon in a skillet, and cook over medium-high heat until it is crisp. Drain on paper towels. When cool enough to handle, crumble it. Add the onions to the bacon drippings in the skillet, and cook, stirring, over medium heat for 3 to 4 minutes. Add the corn, and cook for another 2 to 3 minutes. Remove the skillet from the heat, add the bacon crumbles, and let the vegetables cool to room temperature.

Preheat the oven to 400 degrees. Grease a 9-inch pie pan. In a large bowl whisk together the eggs, cream, milk, and green chilies. Add the corn mixture to the egg mixture along with the cheese, salt, and pepper. Pour the mixture into the pie pan, and bake, uncovered, for 45 minutes. Let the quiche cool for 10 minutes, and then serve it warm or at room temperature.

MAKES 8 SERVINGS.

Great American Brass Band Festival

DANVILLE, KENTUCKY

JUNE

WWW.GABBF.ORG

Every summer some of America's most talented brass band musicians bring their horns, trombones, and cornets to the quaint Kentucky town of Danville. The Great American Brass Band Festival is a long weekend full of music, shopping, and picnicking. The idea behind the festival is to celebrate the culture and history of the American brass band.

The party kicks off on Thursday night with a tea and Gallery Hop to allow festival-goers the chance to shop and explore the adorable downtown area. Friday is a family affair full of brass band music at various venues and the whimsical Hot Air Balloon Race. For those interested in learning more about the history of the American brass band, the brass symposium is the perfect opportunity to do so.

Friday night concludes with a big food and music party called Bayou and Brass, featuring New Orleans–style cuisine and music that will have you dancing the night away. Saturday night, however, is the real opportunity for home cooks to shine during the huge picnic on the lawn where contests are held for the most decorated picnic table. This is truly a one-of-a-kind event that provides something for everyone.

KICKIN' DIRTY RICE

This simple dirty rice gets a kick from spicy andouille, which makes it a definite crowd-pleaser. It pairs wonderfully with barbecued shrimp and corn on the cob.

2 1/2 cups chicken broth, divided

1 cup uncooked white rice

1 tablespoon canola oil

6 ounces smoked andouille, cubed

1 clove garlic, finely chopped

3/4 cup chopped white onion

3/4 cup chopped green bell pepper

1/2 cup chopped celery

1 teaspoon Cajun seasoning

Salt and ground black pepper, to taste

Pour 2 cups of the chicken broth into a medium saucepan, and bring to a boil over high heat. Add the rice, and cook according to package directions. While the rice is cooking, place the oil in a large skillet, and heat over medium-high heat. Add the andouille, and cook until browned, for 2 to 3 minutes. Reduce the heat to medium, and add the garlic, onions, green peppers, and celery to the skillet. Cook until the vegetables have softened, for 6 to 7 minutes.

Add the cooked rice to the skillet along with the Cajun seasoning. Add the remaining 1/2 cup chicken broth, and cook, stirring, over medium heat until the liquid is absorbed. Taste the rice to see if it needs salt and pepper. How much to add will depend on the Cajun seasoning you used. Serve the rice warm or at room temperature.

MAKES 6 TO 8 SERVINGS.

GRUYÈRE GRILLED POTATOES

These fanned potatoes sure aren't lacking for personality with the butter and cheese nestled between each slice. Not only do they taste divine, they make for a beautiful presentation. A potato never looked so good!

4 medium russet potatoes, washed

4 tablespoons cold butter, thinly sliced

4 ounces Gruyère cheese, thinly sliced

2 tablespoons canola oil

1 teaspoon salt

3/4 teaspoon ground black pepper

Heat the grill to medium-high heat. Cut slits in each potato about 1/8 inch apart without cutting all the way through to the bottom. In every other slit insert the butter slices. In the alternating slits insert the cheese. Place each potato on a square of aluminum foil, and drizzle each with the oil. Sprinkle the salt and pepper evenly on each potato as well.

Wrap the potatoes loosely in the foil, and then place them over indirect heat on the grill. Close the grill lid, and cook the potatoes for 45 to 50 minutes, until a fork easily pierces them. Remove them from the grill, carefully open each packet, and serve them hot.

MAKES 4 SERVINGS.

THE FESTIVAL AT SANDPOINT

SANDPOINT, IDAHO
AUGUST
FESTIVALATSANDPOINT.COM

Since the early 1970s, the Festival at Sandpoint in the small town of Sandpoint, Idaho, has been the home to an annual summer concert series with eight nights of eclectic music under the stars on the shores of Lake Pend Oreille. Performances include everyone from the Spokane Symphony to B.B. King, from Tony Bennett to Lyle Lovett.

Best of all, the festival is intimate. It feels as though the arts are playing in your own backyard, a private concert for you and your friends and family. With artists from virtually every genre of music in a given year, the organizers of the Festival at Standpoint want concertgoers to get back to their musical roots in an experience that is both rare and precious.

Attendees can relax on a blanket or in a lawn chair and enjoy their own picnic supper from home or food purchased at the festival.

HAM AND PINEAPPLE SKEWERS

Ham and pineapple is without a doubt one of my favorite food combinations. I just love those sweet and salty flavors, y'all! When you stick those two on skewers, brush them with a brown sugar glaze, and then grill them up, the result is simply irresistible.

1 (12-ounce) ham steak, cut into 1-inch cubes

4 cups 1-inch chunks pineapple (1 large pineapple)

1/2 cup fresh orange juice

1/4 cup firmly packed brown sugar

2 tablespoons spicy brown mustard

Heat the grill to medium-high heat. Thread the ham and pineapple pieces alternately onto wooden skewers. Stir together the orange juice, brown sugar, and mustard in a small bowl. Brush the ham and pineapple with the juice mixture, and then place the skewers on the grill. Cook for 10 minutes, rotating and brushing the glaze on the skewers every 2 to 3 minutes. Serve the skewers hot or at room temperature.

MAKES 4 TO 6 SERVINGS.

Johnny Appleseed Salad

Now, I didn't personally know Johnny Appleseed, but I have a feeling he would have loved this salad. All of the ingredients including the dressing are wonderful complements to the apples.

Maple Glazed Walnuts

1 1/2 cups walnuts

1/3 cup maple syrup

1/4 teaspoon salt

Maple-Dijon Vinaigrette

1/4 cup cider vinegar

1 tablespoon maple syrup

2 teaspoons Dijon mustard

1/4 teaspoon salt

1/4 teaspoon ground black pepper

1/2 cup extra-virgin olive oil

Salad

1 pound mixed greens

1 unpeeled apple, chopped

6 ounces crumbled blue cheese

1/3 cup dried cranberries

For the walnuts, place the walnuts, maple syrup, and salt in a large saucepan over medium-high heat. Cook, stirring constantly, until the syrup begins to thicken, for about 5 minutes. Once the walnuts are fully coated, spread them out onto waxed or parchment paper to cool.

For the vinaigrette, whisk together the vinegar, maple syrup, mustard, salt, and pepper in a small bowl. Slowly drizzle in the oil while whisking until the dressing is emulsified.

When you are ready to serve the salad, place the greens in a large bowl, and add the dressing, tossing everything together to coat well. Top the salad with the apples, walnuts, blue cheese, and cranberries.

Makes 8 servings.

Tip: To travel with this salad, prepare the walnuts and dressing ahead of time. Store all of the salad ingredients separately in airtight containers. Assemble the salad on location just before serving.

Sunshine Carrot and Cranberry Salad

This colorful, cheery salad will brighten up any picnic table. Traditionally it's made with raisins, but I think the cranberries give it a nice tang and pop of red color.

3 cups shredded carrots

2 (8-ounce) cans pineapple tidbits, drained

1/2 cup dried cranberries

1/2 cup mayonnaise

2 tablespoons fresh orange juice

1/4 teaspoon salt

In a serving bowl stir together the carrots, pineapple, and cranberries. In a small bowl whisk together the mayonnaise, orange juice, and salt. Pour the dressing over the carrot mixture, and toss everything together until all of the ingredients are coated. Refrigerate the salad until you are ready to serve it.

MAKES 6 TO 8 SERVINGS.

PEANUTTY CAULIFLOWER SALAD

*Who would have ever thought that peanuts and cauliflower would go so well together.
But don't take my word for it; try this salad. I like to bring it to picnics or barbecues
when other guests have already signed up for all the "staple" side dishes.*

1 head cauliflower

$^1/_2$ cup lightly salted peanuts

$^1/_2$ cup golden raisins

3 tablespoons fresh lemon juice

1 tablespoon honey

2 tablespoons extra-virgin olive oil

2 tablespoons chopped fresh parsley

$^1/_4$ teaspoon salt

$^1/_4$ teaspoon ground black pepper

Break off or cut the cauliflower into small florets. Place the florets in a large bowl, and add the peanuts and raisins. In a small bowl whisk together the lemon juice, honey, oil, parsley, salt, and pepper. Pour the dressing over the salad, and toss everything together until it is well coated. Serve the dish at room temperature, or refrigerate until you are ready to serve it.

MAKES 4 TO 6 SERVINGS.

CUCUMBER AND TOMATO ORZO

If you do much gardening or ever go to a farmers' market during the summer, you will find an abundance of tomatoes and cucumbers. I am always looking for ways to use up my grandmother's never-ending supply of tomatoes, and this salad does the trick. It's simple, colorful, and gets more flavorful as it sits.

1 cup uncooked orzo pasta

1 1/2 cups chopped and seeded cucumber

1 1/2 cups chopped and seeded tomatoes

2 tablespoons red wine vinegar

2 tablespoons extra-virgin olive oil

1 tablespoon finely chopped shallot

2 tablespoons chopped fresh basil

1/2 teaspoon salt

1/2 teaspoon sugar

1/4 teaspoon ground black pepper

Cook the orzo according to the package directions, and then drain it. Place the pasta in a large serving bowl. Add the cucumber, tomatoes, vinegar, oil, shallot, basil, salt, sugar, and pepper to the warm pasta. Toss everything together until it is well combined.

Refrigerate the salad for at least 30 minutes before serving.

MAKES 6 TO 8 SERVINGS.

Shaved Brussels Sprout Slaw

Since Brussels sprouts are the smallest members of the cabbage family, it just makes sense to make slaw out of them. And let me tell you, sprouts never tasted so good—they're coated with bacon drippings, after all!

---

1 pound Brussels sprouts

6 thin slices pancetta

1 shallot, finely chopped

1/2 cup chopped pecans

1 tablespoon fresh lemon juice

2 teaspoons Dijon mustard

1/4 teaspoon salt

1/4 teaspoon ground black pepper

Using a mandoline or sharp knife, slice the Brussels sprouts very thinly, and place them in a bowl. Cook the pancetta in a skillet over medium heat until it is crisp. Drain on paper towels. When cool enough to handle, crumble the pancetta. Add the shallots to the skillet, and cook them over medium heat in the pancetta drippings until they are softened.

Pour the shallots and the drippings over the Brussels sprouts. Add the crumbled pancetta and pecans. In a small bowl whisk together the lemon juice, mustard, salt, and pepper, and pour over the slaw. Toss everything together until it is well coated. Refrigerate the slaw until you are ready to serve it.

MAKES 4 TO 6 SERVINGS.

Muffaletta Tortellini Salad

The famous muffaletta sandwich originated in the French Quarter of New Orleans, and it's known for its strongly flavored Italian meats and cheeses. Since I don't know what's more Italian than tortellini, I've turned the legendary sandwich into a delicious pasta salad.

2 (9-ounce) packages cheese tortellini

1 (14-ounce) can artichoke hearts, drained and chopped

1/4 cup chopped pitted green olives

1/4 cup chopped pitted Kalamata olives

3 ounces salami, sliced into thin strips

1/4 cup chopped fresh basil

1 cup cherry tomatoes, cut into halves

1/2 cup prepared Italian dressing

Cook the tortellini according to the package directions, and then drain them. Place the pasta in a large bowl. Add the artichokes, green olives, Kalamata olives, salami, basil, and cherry tomatoes. Add the Italian dressing, and gently toss everything together until the pasta is well coated. Serve this dish at room temperature, or refrigerate until you are ready to serve it.

MAKES 8 TO 10 SERVINGS.

Charred Caesar Salad

Once you start grilling your salad, you might not ever want it any other way. Romaine lettuce holds up really well on the grill, and this Caesar dressing comes to life over the warm salad.

3 romaine hearts

2 tablespoons fresh lemon juice

1 clove garlic, finely chopped

1 teaspoon Worcestershire sauce

2 teaspoons Dijon mustard

1/8 teaspoon salt

1/4 teaspoon ground black pepper

1/4 cup extra-virgin olive oil

1 cup cherry tomatoes, cut into halves

1/3 cup freshly grated Parmesan cheese

Cut the romaine hearts into halves lengthwise. Whisk together the lemon juice, garlic, Worcestershire sauce, mustard, salt, and pepper in a small bowl. Drizzle in the oil while whisking until the dressing is emulsified.

Heat the grill to high heat. Brush the romaine halves lightly with the dressing, and place them on the grill, cut side down. Cook until the romaine is nicely charred on all sides, rotating the pieces every 2 minutes. Remove them from the grill, and top with the tomatoes and Parmesan. Pour the remaining dressing over the grilled romaine, and serve the salads immediately.

MAKES 6 SERVINGS.

Hoppin' John Salad

Hoppin' John gets a mouthwatering twist with the addition of a warm bacon vinaigrette.

1 medium red bell pepper, chopped

3 celery ribs, chopped

1 cup cooked long-grain rice

2 (15-ounce) cans black-eyed peas, drained and rinsed

5 slices bacon

½ cup chopped red onion

1 tablespoon brown sugar

¼ cup cider vinegar

¼ teaspoon salt

¼ teaspoon ground black pepper

In a large serving bowl stir together the red peppers, celery, rice, and peas. Cook the bacon in a skillet until it is crisp. Drain on paper towels. Reserve 3 tablespoons of the bacon drippings in the skillet. Crumble the bacon when it is cool enough to handle.

Add the onions and brown sugar to the drippings, and cook over medium heat until the onions have slightly softened, for 2 to 3 minutes. Add the vinegar to the skillet. Pour the bacon drippings and onion mixture over the peas and rice. Add the crumbled bacon, salt, and pepper, and stir everything together until all of the ingredients are well coated. Serve the dish at room temperature, or refrigerate and serve chilled.

Makes 6 to 8 servings.

WOLF TRAP

VIENNA, VIRGINIA
CHECK CALENDAR FOR CONCERT LISTINGS
WOLFTRAP.ORG

Wolf Trap, as it is known to Washington, D.C., locals, is actually officially known as the Wolf Trap National Park for the Performing Arts. This 130-acre haven for the arts ensures that the arts remain accessible and affordable to the broadest possible audience.

A typical season at Wolf Trap includes something for everyone with performances ranging from pop, country, folk, and blues to orchestra, dance, theatre, and opera, as well as innovative performance art and multimedia presentations. Outdoor performances are held in the Filene Center from May through September and at the Barns at Wolf Trap year-round.

While food for purchase is an option at Wolf Trap, guests are permitted to bring their own picnic baskets to enjoy during any of a hundred or so performances held each summer.

GRILLED WATERMELON WITH SWEET BALSAMIC SYRUP

With the abundance of fresh watermelon during the summertime, it's easy to get creative in using the sweet melon. Grilling watermelon allows it to caramelize, and the balsamic syrup adds a punch of tangy flavor.

¹/₂ cup balsamic vinegar	6 cups 2-inch cubes watermelon
1 tablespoon honey	¹/₂ cup crumbled blue cheese
¹/₂ teaspoon finely grated orange peel	

Place the balsamic vinegar, honey, and orange peel in a small saucepan, and bring the mixture to a low simmer over medium heat. Cook until the vinegar is reduced by half. It should have a syrupy consistency.

Heat the grill to medium-high heat. Once the grill is hot, grill the watermelon cubes for about 2 minutes, turn, and grill for 2 more minutes, or until grill marks are formed. Place the melon on a large serving plate, and drizzle with the reduced vinegar. Sprinkle with blue cheese, and serve immediately.

MAKES 6 SERVINGS.

Garlic Butter
Grilled Asparagus

*Something about asparagus always feels fancy to me, so if you're looking for
a simple side dish for elegant outdoor dining, this one will fit the bill.*

¹/₄ cup (¹/₂ stick) butter	1 ¹/₂ pounds asparagus, trimmed
2 cloves garlic, finely chopped	1 tablespoon extra-virgin olive oil
1 teaspoon finely grated lemon peel	¹/₂ teaspoon salt
2 tablespoons fresh lemon juice	¹/₄ teaspoon ground black pepper

Place the butter in a skillet, and heat over medium heat until melted. Add the garlic and lemon peel to the butter, and cook, stirring constantly, for 1 minute. Remove the skillet from the heat, and then whisk in the lemon juice.

Heat the grill to medium-high heat. Place the asparagus in a bowl and toss with the oil, salt, and pepper. Grill for 6 to 8 minutes, rotating every 2 minutes. Toss the asparagus in a bowl with the butter mixture. Serve warm.

MAKES 6 SERVINGS.

GRILLED "TWICE BAKED" WHITE CHEDDAR POTATOES

Oh, the stories I have heard from my husband about twice-baked potatoes from his childhood. We would have them every night if it was up to him. These are a little different from the ones we grew up with, but they certainly aren't lacking in the ooey-gooey cheesy department!

4 large russet potatoes, washed and dried

4 to 5 slices bacon

¹/₂ cup chopped leeks, white and light green parts only

¹/₂ cup sour cream

¹/₄ cup milk

1 cup freshly shredded white Cheddar cheese, divided

1 /2 cup (1 stick) butter, melted, divided

¹/₂ teaspoon salt

¹/₂ teaspoon ground black pepper

Preheat the oven to 400 degrees. Using a fork, prick the potatoes. Bake them directly on the oven rack until they are fork-tender, for about 1 hour. Let the potatoes cool for 10 minutes, and then cut them into halves lengthwise. Scoop the flesh of the potatoes into a bowl, leaving about ¹/₄-inch thickness around the skin. Mash the potatoes until they are smooth.

Cook the bacon in a skillet over medium-high heat until it is crisp. Drain on paper towels. Crumble the bacon. Reserve 1 tablespoon of the bacon drippings in the skillet. Add the leeks to the drippings, and cook over medium heat until they are softened. Stir the leeks into the potatoes along with the sour cream, milk, 3/4 cup of the cheese, ¹/₄ cup of the butter, salt, and pepper. Spoon the potato mixture back into the potato skins, and top each with some of the remaining cheese and 1 tablespoon butter.

Heat half of the grill to medium-high heat. Place the stuffed potatoes over indirect heat, and close the grill lid. Grill the potatoes for 20 minutes, or until they are warm throughout and the cheese has melted. Serve the potatoes immediately.

If using an oven, bake the stuffed potatoes at 350 degrees for 20 to 25 minutes.

MAKES 8 SERVINGS.

SALAD ON A STICK

This recipe has all of my favorite components of a crisp chef's salad—on a stick. This recipe is picnic-style at its best! Try not to skimp on the fresh herbs in the dressing; they really make all the difference.

CREAMY HERB DRESSING

1 cup mayonnaise

1/2 cup sour cream

1 tablespoon chopped fresh dill

1 tablespoon chopped fresh basil

1 tablespoon chopped fresh chives

1/4 cup cider vinegar

3 tablespoons water

1/2 teaspoon salt

1/2 teaspoon ground black pepper

SALAD

1 head iceberg lettuce

1 baguette

6 large hard-boiled eggs

6 ounces thick sliced turkey

1 pint cherry tomatoes

1 English cucumber, sliced into 1/2-inch coins

6 ounces cubed Cheddar cheese

Long skewers

To make the creamy herb dressing, in a medium bowl stir together the mayonnaise, sour cream, dill, basil, chives, vinegar, water, salt, and pepper. Chill the dressing until you are ready to serve the salad.

To make the salad, chop the lettuce into 2-inch chunks, leaving the lettuce layered together. Cut the baguette into 2-inch pieces as well. Halve the eggs lengthwise, and cut the turkey into 1-inch squares.

To assemble the skewers, place a section of lettuce, a tomato, a piece of baguette, a cucumber slice, an egg half, 2 pieces of turkey, and a cube of cheese on the skewer. Continue skewering in this order until you run out of room on the skewers. When all of the skewers are done, serve them chilled with the dressing on the side or drizzled over the top.

MAKES 6 TO 8 SERVINGS.

ASPARAGUS AND HAM FETTUCCINE SALAD

I had the privilege of working as a sales associate for a gourmet fresh pasta company in Nashville for a while. During that time I learned so much about pasta, and I really began to appreciate fresh pasta in particular. It is absolutely delicious in this chilled fettuccine salad.

1 pound asparagus

1 tablespoon plus ½ teaspoon salt, divided

9 ounces fresh fettuccine

½ cup mayonnaise

2 tablespoons extra-virgin olive oil

2 tablespoons fresh lemon juice

¼ cup freshly grated Parmesan cheese

¼ teaspoon ground black pepper

4 ounces small diced ham

Trim the ends of the asparagus, and cut the spears into 2-inch pieces. Bring a pot of water and 1 tablespoon of the salt to a boil. Add the asparagus, and cook for 2 to 3 minutes. Using tongs, remove the asparagus from the water, and place it in a bowl of ice water to stop the cooking process. Add the pasta to the boiling water, and cook according to the package directions.

In a large bowl whisk together the mayonnaise, oil, lemon juice, Parmesan, remaining ½ teaspoon salt, and pepper. Drain the pasta, and add it to the bowl. Toss until the pasta is well coated with the dressing. Stir in the asparagus and the ham. Refrigerate the dish until you are ready to serve it.

MAKES 4 SERVINGS.

BACK PORCH WHITE MAC AND CHEESE

In every family certain dishes are assigned to the same people year after year. At our family gatherings my grandmother was always the one to make the baked mac and cheese, a favorite of the kids. It was usually paired with barbecued chicken and Jell-O, a delightful trio if you ask me!

12 ounces uncooked elbow macaroni

6 to 8 slices bacon

1/2 cup chopped white onion

1/4 cup (1/2 stick) butter

1/4 cup all-purpose flour

3 1/2 cups whole milk

1 teaspoon salt

3/4 teaspoon ground black pepper

2 cups freshly shredded sharp white Cheddar cheese

1 cup freshly shredded Swiss cheese

1/2 cup freshly grated Parmesan cheese

Cook the macaroni according to the package directions, drain it, and set it aside. Cook the bacon in a large skillet over medium-high heat until it is crisp. Drain on paper towels. Crumble the bacon when cool enough to handle. Reserve 1 tablespoon of the bacon drippings in the skillet. Add the onions to the drippings, and cook over medium-low heat, stirring occasionally, until golden, for 12 to 15 minutes.

Preheat the oven to 350 degrees. Grease a 13 x 9-inch baking dish.

Increase the heat to medium, and add the butter to the onions. Add the flour, and cook, whisking constantly, over medium heat for 2 minutes. Slowly whisk in the milk until there are no lumps. Add the salt and pepper, and cook the sauce until it has thickened, for 8 to 10 minutes.

Remove the skillet from the heat. Add the Cheddar, Swiss, and Parmesan cheeses to the sauce, and stir until they have melted. Add the cooked macaroni and bacon crumbles, and stir until the pasta is well coated. Pour the macaroni mixture into the baking dish, and bake for 30 to 35 minutes, until the top is golden brown and bubbly.

MAKES 10 TO 12 SERVINGS.

GRILLED ZUCCHINI WEDGES WITH SOUR CREAM AND SHALLOT DIP

If you are a sour cream and onion dip lover, then this homemade version will be right up your alley. To give the zucchini some extra zing, let it marinate in the lemon and oil mixture for an hour or so before grilling.

6 medium zucchini, sliced into quarters lengthwise

2 tablespoons fresh lemon juice

2 tablespoons canola oil, divided

1 teaspoon salt, divided

3/4 teaspoon ground black pepper, divided

3 shallots, finely chopped

1 cup sour cream

2 tablespoons sliced green onions

2 teaspoons Worcestershire sauce

Place the zucchini in a large bowl, and toss with the lemon juice, 1 tablespoon of the oil, 3/4 teaspoon of the salt, and 1/2 teaspoon of the pepper. Place a small skillet over medium-low heat, and add the remaining 1 tablespoon oil. Add the shallots to the oil, and cook, stirring occasionally, until they are golden, for 8 to 10 minutes. In a medium bowl mix together the cooked shallots, sour cream, green onions, and Worcestershire sauce.

Heat the grill to medium-high heat. Place the zucchini spears on the grill, and cook them for 3 to 4 minute per side, until they are nicely charred. Serve them warm with the dipping sauce.

MAKES 4 TO 6 SERVINGS.

Fresh Corn Pudding

Corn pudding is a delicious casserole we have at almost every big gathering in my family. It is popular during the holidays, but I think it is delicious made with fresh corn in the summertime too. It does not have to be served piping hot, so it works well for a porch gathering.

3 tablespoons butter

2 cups fresh corn kernels (may substitute frozen)

2 green onions, sliced

2 large eggs

1 (12-ounce) can evaporated milk

$^1/_2$ cup sour cream

$^1/_4$ cup yellow cornmeal

1 tablespoon sugar

1 teaspoon salt

$^1/_2$ teaspoon ground black pepper

$^1/_2$ cup shredded sharp Cheddar cheese

Preheat the oven to 350 degrees. Grease a 9-inch square baking dish. Place the butter in a skillet over medium heat, and heat until melted. Add the corn and green onions, and cook until the corn has slightly softened, for 4 to 5 minutes. Remove the skillet from the heat, and set it aside to cool.

In a large bowl whisk together the eggs, milk, and sour cream until there are no lumps. Whisk in the cornmeal, sugar, salt, and pepper. Add the slightly cooled corn mixture to the milk mixture, and stir until well combined. Pour the mixture into the baking dish.

Bake the pudding for 30 minutes. Sprinkle the cheese evenly on top, and then bake it for another 10 minutes. Remove the dish from the oven, let it cool slightly, and serve warm or at room temperature.

MAKES 6 TO 8 SERVINGS.

RAVINIA

HIGHLAND PARK, ILLINOIS
JUNE THROUGH SEPTEMBER
RAVINIA.ORG

More than 600,000 folks visit this Chicago burb every summer to watch jazz and classical music performances as well as musical theater productions. The summer home to the Chicago Symphony Orchestra, Ravinia holds 120 to 150 events each year.

Enjoying a picnic while listening to a concert under the stars at this venue is as much a part of summer in the Chicago area as watching the Cubs play baseball.

Guests are encouraged to bring tables and chairs and blankets to share a picnic supper on the lawn before venturing into the Pavilion to enjoy music under the stars.

CHEDDAR MAC AND CHEESE CUPS

You know how the best part of baked macaroni and cheese are those crunchy edges? Well, these individual baked mac and cheese cups give you a little bit of that cheesy crust in almost every bite. A serving size of these is about two cups per person, but you may want to make extra for a hungry crowd.

Cooking spray

2 cups uncooked elbow macaroni

3 tablespoons butter, divided

2 ounces cream cheese

1 cup low-fat or whole milk

1 large egg, beaten

2 cups freshly shredded sharp Cheddar cheese

1/4 teaspoon salt

1/4 teaspoon ground black pepper

1/2 cup panko bread crumbs

Preheat the oven to 350 degrees, and spray a 12-cup muffin tin with cooking spray. Cook the macaroni according to the package directions. Drain it, and place in a large bowl. Stir in 2 tablespoons of the butter and the cream cheese until they begin to melt into the warm pasta. Add the milk, egg, Cheddar cheese, salt, and pepper, and stir until everything is well blended. The cheese does not have to be completely melted at this point. Spoon the mixture evenly into the muffin tin, making sure to add any remaining liquid to the cups as well.

Melt the remaining 1 tablespoon butter in the microwave or on the stovetop. Place it in a small bowl, and toss it with the panko. Sprinkle evenly over each cup. Bake for 30 minutes. Let the cups cool for 5 minutes before removing them from the tin. Serve warm.

MAKES 12 SERVINGS.

TIP: You can make these in mini muffin tins as well for a bite-size treat. Follow the directions as listed, but bake the mini cups for 12 to 15 minutes. Makes 48 mini muffin cups.

HOMINY SOUTHERN SUCCOTASH

This simple summer comfort food recipe will surprise you with different textures. Of course, any vegetable side dish cooked in bacon drippings is usually a winner, and this one is no exception. Since we are hominy lovers in my house, adding it to a classic succotash was a no-brainer for me.

---

1 (10-ounce) package frozen baby lima beans

4 slices bacon

1 cup chopped sweet onion

2 ears of corn, shucked

1 (16-ounce) can golden hominy, drained

1 teaspoon sugar

1/2 teaspoon salt

1/2 teaspoon ground black pepper

Cook the lima beans in boiling water, according to the package directions, and then drain them. Place the bacon in a large skillet over medium-high heat, and cook it until crisp. Drain on paper towels, and let cool. Add the onions to the drippings in the skillet, and cook until they begin to soften, for 5 to 6 minutes. Add the corn, and cook for another 3 to 4 minutes. Add the lima beans, hominy, sugar, salt, and pepper, and stir until well combined. Crumble the bacon and add to the mixture. Continue cooking until all of the vegetables are heated through. Serve warm or at room temperature.

MAKES 6 TO 8 SERVINGS.

SUMMER SQUASH AND RICE CASSEROLE

Cheesy squash casserole is a familiar and comforting summertime treat. This recipe calls for cooked rice, which gives the dish a nice hearty texture, and it's a great way to use up leftover rice.

Cooking spray

4 medium yellow squash, chopped into ¹/₂-inch pieces

4 tablespoons butter, divided

1 cup chopped white onion

1 cup cooked long-grain rice

1 cup sour cream

1 cup freshly shredded Cheddar cheese

1 ¹/₄ teaspoons salt, divided

¹/₂ teaspoon ground black pepper

1 tablespoon finely chopped fresh chives

1 tablespoon chopped fresh parsley

¹/₂ cup dry bread crumbs

Preheat the oven to 350 degrees, and spray a 2-quart baking dish with cooking spray. Bring a large pot of water to a boil, and add the chopped squash. Boil for 5 minutes, drain, and place the squash in a large bowl. Melt 2 tablespoons of the butter in a saucepan over medium heat. Add the onions, and cook until they have softened, for 6 to 8 minutes. Add the onions to the squash. Add the rice, sour cream, cheese, 1 teaspoon of the salt, and the pepper. Toss everything together, and pour it into the baking dish.

Melt the remaining 2 tablespoons butter in the microwave or on the stovetop. Pour butter into a small bowl, and toss it with the chives, parsley, bread crumbs, and the remaining ¹/₄ teaspoon salt. Sprinkle the crumb mixture over the squash mixture. Bake the dish for 30 minutes. Serve warm.

MAKES 6 TO 8 SERVINGS.

SPARKLING BERRY CONGEALED SALAD

This simple Jell-O salad pairs well with grilled meats and barbecue. The ginger ale really gives it a nice boost.

3 (3-ounce) packages raspberry gelatin

3 cups boiling water

3 cups cold ginger ale

3 cups frozen mixed berries

2 teaspoons finely grated orange peel

3/4 cup chopped pecans

Place the gelatin in a large bowl, and add the boiling water. Stir until the gelatin is completely dissolved. Stir in the ginger ale. Refrigerate the gelatin for 30 minutes, until it is slightly firm but still runny.

Stir the berries, orange peel, and pecans into the gelatin mixture. Pour it into a mold, if desired. Refrigerate the salad for at least 4 hours before serving.

MAKES 10 TO 12 SERVINGS.

TIP: If you are traveling with this dish, be sure to keep it covered and very chilled.

Quick Bread and Butter Pickles

Sweet bread and butter pickles are not only a tasty burger or sandwich condiment, they also make a yummy snack. If you want to make some in a pinch, here's a recipe that won't take much time but still offers all the flavor of the traditional pickle. And remember: the fresher the cucumber, the crispier the pickles.

6 Kirby cucumbers

1/2 cup white vinegar

1/2 cup cider vinegar

2 tablespoons brown sugar

1 1/2 teaspoons salt

1 white onion, thinly sliced

2 cloves garlic, crushed

1 teaspoon mustard seeds

1 teaspoon allspice berries

1/4 teaspoon crushed red pepper flakes

Slice the cucumbers into 1/2-inch slices, and place them in a large sealable container. Put the white vinegar, cider vinegar, brown sugar, salt, onions, garlic, mustard seeds, allspice berries, and red pepper flakes in a medium saucepan, and bring to a boil over high heat. Cook until the sugar and salt have dissolved. Pour the vinegar mixture over the sliced cucumbers. If the cucumbers are not fully submerged, cover them with cold water. Refrigerate the pickles for at least 1 hour before serving.

MAKES 1 1/2 PINTS.

CITRUS AND MINT GRAIN SALAD

This hearty salad gets a citrus twist from the fresh orange and grapefruit. The mint also adds a clean flavor, and the pecans give it that perfect crunch.

1 cup uncooked bulgur

2 cups low-sodium chicken broth

1 teaspoon finely grated orange peel

1/4 cup fresh orange juice

2 tablespoons extra-virgin olive oil

3/4 teaspoon salt

1/2 teaspoon ground black pepper

1 orange, peeled and segmented

1/2 large grapefruit, peeled and segmented

1/2 cup feta cheese crumbles

1/4 cup chopped pecans

2 tablespoons chopped fresh mint

Cook the bulgur according to the package directions, using the chicken broth instead of water. Put in a bowl, and let cool to room temperature. In a small bowl whisk together the orange peel, orange juice, oil, salt, and pepper. Pour the dressing over the bulgur, and add the orange and grapefruit segments, the feta, pecans, and mint. Toss everything together until the bulgur and fruit are well coated. Refrigerate the salad until you are ready to serve it.

MAKES 4 TO 6 SERVINGS.

GRILLED EGGPLANT
CANAPÉS

I didn't grow up eating much eggplant, but after seeing them at farmers' markets year after year, I have grown to love them. Their hearty texture makes them great for grilling, and this is a beautiful way to dress them up with some ricotta and garden-fresh cherry tomatoes.

1 large eggplant, unpeeled

1 cup ricotta cheese

4 ounces goat cheese, softened

3 tablespoons extra-virgin olive oil, divided

1 tablespoon balsamic vinegar

1 cup cherry tomatoes, cut into halves

3/4 teaspoon salt

1/2 teaspoon ground black pepper

Slice the eggplant into 1/4-inch slices. In a small bowl mix together the ricotta and goat cheeses. In a medium bowl stir together 1 tablespoon of the olive oil and the balsamic vinegar. Add the cherry tomatoes, and toss until they are well coated.

Heat the grill to medium-high heat. Brush the eggplant slices with the remaining 2 tablespoons oil, and sprinkle them with the salt and pepper. Grill the eggplant for 3 to 4 minutes per side, until grill marks have formed. Transfer the eggplant to a serving platter, and top each slice with a spoonful of the cheese mixture and a couple of the tomatoes. Serve immediately.

MAKES ABOUT 16 SERVINGS.

STRAWBERRY POPPY SEED SPINACH SALAD

This salad is light and fresh with a pretty pop of color from the strawberries.
The addition of the arugula adds a touch of spice to this sweet salad.

POPPY SEED DRESSING

1/2 cup mayonnaise

2 tablespoons fresh lemon juice

1 tablespoon honey

1 1/2 teaspoons poppy seeds

1/4 teaspoon salt

SALAD

5 ounces baby spinach

1 cup arugula, packed

2 cups sliced strawberries

6 slices bacon, cooked and crumbled

1/2 cup chopped walnuts

For the dressing, in a small bowl whisk together the mayonnaise, lemon juice, honey, poppy seeds, and salt.

For the salad, toss together the spinach and arugula in a large serving bowl. Top the greens with the strawberries, bacon, and walnuts. Drizzle some of the dressing on top of the salad, and toss until the greens are coated. Serve the remaining dressing on the side.

MAKES 6 SERVINGS.

MOONLIGHT MOVIES

PEACE CENTER AMPHITHEATRE
GREENVILLE, SOUTH CAROLINA
WEDNESDAYS, MAY THROUGH SEPTEMBER
WWW.GREENVILLESC.GOV

Greenville, South Carolina, is a hip, Southern town nestled in the foothills of the Blue Ridge Mountains. There is no shortage of activities and events downtown, including Moonlight Movies, which take place at the Peace Center Amphitheatre during the summers.

You won't find the newest releases at this outdoor theatre. This is family-friendly affair featuring classic films from the 1950s, '60s, and '70s. The free event is a fantastic opportunity for the kids to meet some of silver screen's most memorable characters such as "the Duke" and maybe even those silly Three Stooges. Bring a themed picnic based on the movie being shown; you might just feel as if you've stepped back into "the good ole days."

Pink Beet Potato Salad

This eye-catching potato salad is so unique, and it's not every day you get to make a pink side dish. The texture and slightly sweet flavor of the roasted beets is a wonderful complement to the new potatoes.

3 medium red beets, trimmed

1 tablespoon canola oil

1 pound new potatoes

1/3 cup mayonnaise

1 tablespoon fresh lemon juice

1/2 cup finely chopped celery

1/4 cup plus 1 tablespoon sliced green onions, divided

1 teaspoon salt

3/4 teaspoon ground black pepper

Preheat the oven to 400 degrees. Drizzle the beets with the oil, wrap them in aluminum foil, and bake them for 1 hour. Let them cool for 10 minutes, and then peel them. Cut the beets into 1 1/2-inch cubes.

Place the potatoes in a large pot, and cover them with water. Bring the water to a boil over high heat, and cook the potatoes until they are tender, for 12 to 14 minutes. Drain the potatoes, and let them cool slightly before cutting them into quarters.

In a large bowl mix together the mayonnaise, lemon juice, celery, 1/4 cup of the green onions, salt, and pepper. Place the cooked beets and the potatoes in the bowl, and gently toss everything together until the vegetables are completely coated and the mixture turns pink. Top the salad with the remaining 1 tablespoon green onions. Refrigerate the salad until you are ready to serve it.

MAKES 6 TO 8 SERVINGS.

MAIN
DISHES

PECAN-CRUSTED CHICKEN BITES WITH MAPLE MUSTARD SAUCE

When my grandparents talk about their memories of outdoor church potlucks, they recall their mothers always bringing homemade fried chicken. It didn't matter that it wasn't piping hot; fried chicken was always part of the picnic spread. Nowadays chicken nuggets seem to be the staple, so this is my simple version of crispy chicken that is delicious served hot or at room temperature.

CHICKEN BITES

Cooking spray

1 1/2 pounds chicken breast, cut into 2-inch nuggets

1 /2 cup all-purpose flour

2 large eggs

1 cup finely crushed pecans

1 cup panko bread crumbs

1 1/4 teaspoons salt

1 teaspoon ground black pepper

MAPLE MUSTARD SAUCE

2 tablespoons honey

2 tablespoons maple syrup

1 tablespoon Dijon mustard

1/2 teaspoon chili powder

1/4 teaspoon salt

For the chicken, preheat the oven to 375 degrees. Place a wire rack on a baking sheet, and spray it with cooking spray. Place the chicken nuggets in a bowl, and add the flour. Toss until the chicken is well coated. In a shallow dish beat the eggs, and in another shallow dish combine the pecans, panko, salt, and pepper. Dip the chicken into the egg and then into the pecan mixture, working in batches until all of the chicken is well coated.

Place the chicken on the rack, making sure that the pieces are not touching. Spray liberally with cooking spray. Bake the chicken for 12 to 15 minutes, until it is golden and cooked through.

For the sauce, in a small bowl stir together the honey, maple syrup, mustard, chili powder, and salt. Serve the sauce alongside the chicken nuggets. If you are traveling with this dish, store the sauce separately from the nuggets until you are ready to serve them.

MAKES 6 SERVINGS.

TIP: Serve these chicken nuggets on a platter with toothpicks for everyone to snack on.

ROLL TIDE WHITE BARBECUED CHICKEN

If you are an Alabama native, you have probably grown up on white barbecue sauce.
It sounds slightly odd to the rest of us, but when you baste this creamy white sauce
on grilled chicken, something magical happens. The moisture of the chicken is sealed
in by the tangy white sauce, adding a unique flavor that perfectly complements
the charred meat. This just might be one of Alabama's best-kept secrets!

4 pounds bone-in, skin-on chicken pieces

2 tablespoons canola oil

1 1/2 tablespoons Cajun seasoning

1 cup mayonnaise

1/4 cup cider vinegar

1 tablespoon fresh lemon juice

2 teaspoons prepared horseradish

1 teaspoon sugar

1/2 teaspoon onion powder

1/2 teaspoon garlic powder

1/2 teaspoon salt

1/4 teaspoon ground black pepper, or to taste

Heat the grill to medium-high heat. Put the chicken pieces in a bowl, and coat them with the oil and Cajun seasoning. In a small bowl whisk together the mayonnaise, vinegar, lemon juice, horseradish, sugar, onion powder, garlic powder, salt, and pepper.

Place the chicken pieces on the grill, and close the lid. Grill the chicken for 4 to 5 minutes per side, and then turn the burners off on one side of the grill. Move the chicken pieces to the indirect heat, and baste them with the sauce. Close the lid, and cook for another 10 to 12 minutes, turning and basting the chicken occasionally. Serve the chicken hot off the grill.

Makes 6 servings.

Tip: If you are preparing this chicken for a tailgate, coat the chicken in the oil and seasonings, and prepare the sauce separately. Grill and baste with sauce at the venue.

Pork Tenderloin
and Pineapple Slaw
Sweet Rolls

Instead of the usual pulled pork or ribs at your next gathering, try these adorable pork tenderloin sliders for a refreshing change. Make the day of your gathering a breeze by preparing the slaw the night before and marinating the pork overnight for an extra smoky flavor.

Pork Tenderloin

1/2 cup fresh lime juice

2 tablespoons brown sugar

1 1/2 teaspoons ground cumin

3 cloves garlic, crushed

2 teaspoons Worcestershire sauce

1/2 teaspoon salt

1/2 teaspoon ground black pepper

2 pounds pork tenderloin, trimmed

Pineapple Slaw

1 (14-ounce) package coleslaw mix

1 (8-ounce) can pineapple tidbits, 1/4 cup of the juice reserved

1 red bell pepper, seeded and chopped

1/2 cup sliced green onions

1/4 cup fresh lime juice

1/4 cup mayonnaise

2 teaspoons honey

3/4 teaspoon salt

1/2 teaspoon ground black pepper

Sandwiches

1 (12-count) package sweet dinner rolls

1 cup prepared barbecue sauce

For the pork, in a 13 x 9-inch glass baking dish whisk together the lime juice, brown sugar, cumin, garlic, Worcestershire sauce, salt, and pepper. Add the pork, and roll in the marinade a few times to coat. Cover the dish, and refrigerate for at least 2 hours or overnight.

For the slaw, in a large bowl toss together the coleslaw mix, pineapple, red peppers, and green onions. In a small bowl whisk together the reserved pineapple juice, lime juice, mayonnaise, honey, salt, and pepper. Pour the dressing over the slaw mixture, and stir to coat the slaw completely. Refrigerate the slaw for at least 30 minutes.

Heat the grill to medium heat. Remove the pork from the marinade, pat dry with paper towels, and place on the grill. Cook for 12 to 15 minutes, with the grill lid closed, rotating the pork every 3 to 4 minutes. Remove the pork from the grill, and let it rest for 5 minutes.

Slice the pork into 1-inch slices. Split the rolls, and place a slice of pork on the bottom half of each roll. Top with the barbecue sauce and slaw, and then top with the other half of the roll. Continue assembling the sandwiches until all of the pork and rolls have been used. Serve immediately.

Makes 12 servings.

Crab Cake Sliders with Spicy Remoulade Sauce

These mini crab cake sammies will be the first to go at your next porch party. The presentation is fantastic, and crab cakes will be an unexpected treat at an outdoor event. The remoulade sauce keeps the sliders moist as well as adding the perfect amount of spice to this elegant finger food.

Remoulade Sauce

$1/2$ cup mayonnaise

2 tablespoons spicy brown mustard

2 teaspoons hot pepper sauce

2 tablespoons sweet pickle relish

2 teaspoons fresh lemon juice

$1/2$ teaspoon salt

$1/4$ teaspoon ground black pepper

$1/4$ teaspoon garlic powder

Crab Cakes

1 pound crab claw meat

2 large eggs

1 $1/2$ cups soft bread crumbs

$1/2$ cup finely chopped celery

$1/2$ cup chopped green onions

2 tablespoons spicy brown mustard

3 teaspoons Worcestershire sauce

2 teaspoons Old Bay seasoning

2 teaspoons finely grated lemon peel

1 tablespoon canola oil

1 (16-count) package mini Parker House rolls

For the sauce, in a small bowl stir together the mayonnaise, mustard, hot pepper sauce, relish, lemon juice, salt, pepper, and garlic powder.

For the crab cakes, in a large bowl mix together the crabmeat, eggs, bread crumbs, celery, green onions, mustard, Worcestershire sauce, Old Bay seasoning, and lemon peel in a medium bowl. Form 16 balls out of the crab mixture, and then slightly flatten each one.

In a large skillet heat the canola oil over medium-high heat. Add the crab cakes in batches, and fry them until they are golden brown, for 2 to 3 minutes per side. Remove the cakes from the skillet, and drain on paper towels. Repeat this process until all of the crab cakes are cooked.

Heat the rolls according to the package directions, and then split them into halves. Place a crab cake on the bottom of each roll.

Spoon some of the remoulade sauce on top of the crab cake, and then place the roll top over the sauce. Stick a long toothpick through the sandwich to hold it together. Repeat this process until all the crab cakes and rolls have been used.

MAKES 16 SERVINGS.

TIP: Make the crab cakes ahead of time, and then reheat them in a 300-degree oven on a baking sheet before assembling the sandwiches.

Mustard-Herb Grilled Pork Chops

My father-in-law's marinated pork chops are a treat we look forward to every summer. He has figured out that since pork chops are pretty lean, marinating them is important to give them flavor and keep them from drying out on the grill. The fresh herbs and mustard give this pork recipe a zesty flavor, and the brown sugar helps the pork caramelize on the grill.

1/4 cup Dijon mustard

1 tablespoon brown sugar

1 1/2 teaspoons chopped fresh thyme

1 1/2 teaspoons chopped fresh rosemary

1 tablespoon fresh lemon juice

2 cloves garlic, finely chopped

3/4 teaspoon salt

1/2 teaspoon ground black pepper

4 bone-in pork chops, 1 inch thick

Mix together the mustard, brown sugar, thyme, rosemary, lemon juice, garlic, salt, and pepper. Place the pork chops in a ziptop bag, and pour the mustard mixture over the meat. Seal the bag, and move the meat around inside the bag, making sure each side is coated. Marinate the pork in the refrigerator for at least 1 hour or overnight.

Heat the grill to medium-high heat. Place the pork chops on the grill, and cook for 6 to 8 minutes on each side, turning once. Serve the pork chops hot off the grill.

MAKES 4 SERVINGS.

Lowcountry Shrimp and Sausage Skewers

If you love the flavors of a Lowcountry boil, these grilled skewers will be right up your alley. Spicy sausage and zesty shrimp get fantastic flavor from a lemony Old Bay marinade, brightened up with fresh basil.

1 pound large shrimp, shells removed and tails intact

1 pound Kielbasa sausage, cut into 1-inch pieces

2 tablespoons fresh lemon juice

2 tablespoons canola oil

2 cloves garlic, finely chopped

2 teaspoons Old Bay seasoning

1 tablespoon chopped fresh basil

Thread the shrimp and sausage pieces alternately onto skewers, and place them in a shallow baking dish. In a small bowl mix together the lemon juice, oil, garlic, Old Bay seasoning, and basil. Pour the dressing over the skewers, and marinate for 30 minutes.

Heat the grill to medium-high heat. Place the skewers on the grill, and cook for about 3 minutes on each side, until the shrimp are pink and grill marks have formed. Serve the skewers hot off the grill.

Makes 4 to 6 servings.

TIP: If using wooden skewers, soak them in water for 30 minutes prior to assembling.

CHARRED APPLE-PECAN CHICKEN SALAD

When I first met my husband, I had to learn pretty quickly how to make a good chicken salad. I was always trying to recreate the version that he loved most from a deli near his grandparents' house. Since most of us have a favorite traditional version of this classic picnic salad, I decided to change it up by grilling the chicken and adding everyone's favorite ingredient: bacon. You can make sandwiches out of this or serve it as a salad over lettuce.

---

2 teaspoons chopped fresh thyme

1 teaspoon finely grated lemon peel

3 tablespoons fresh lemon juice

1 tablespoon canola oil

1/2 teaspoon salt

1/4 teaspoon ground black pepper

1 1/2 pounds boneless, skinless chicken breast halves

1 cup chopped, peeled Granny Smith apples

1/2 cup chopped toasted pecans

6 slices bacon, cooked and chopped

1/2 cup chopped celery

1 cup light mayonnaise

Ground black pepper (optional)

In a large bowl mix together the thyme, lemon peel, lemon juice, oil, salt, and pepper. Add the chicken, and toss to coat. Cover and marinate the chicken in the refrigerator for at least 1 hour or overnight.

Heat the grill to medium-high heat. Place the chicken on the grill, and cook for 7 to 8 minutes per side, until it is cooked through. Remove the chicken from the grill, and let it cool slightly. Chop the chicken into bite-size pieces. In a large bowl combine the chicken, apples, pecans, bacon, and celery. Add the mayonnaise, and stir to coat all of the ingredients. Add the pepper to taste. Refrigerate the salad until you are ready to serve it.

MAKES 4 TO 6 SERVINGS.

Buffalo Chicken Tenders with Gorgonzola Dipping Sauce

I made this dish for the first time during football season a few years ago, and it was a huge hit. A tailgating feast just isn't complete anymore without these chicken tenders on the menu. The spiciness of the chicken paired with the cool, tangy Gorgonzola dip is a classic combination.

Gorgonzola Dip

6 ounces Gorgonzola cheese

1/2 cup buttermilk

1/2 cup light mayonnaise

2 tablespoons Dijon mustard

1/2 teaspoon salt

1/2 teaspoon ground black pepper

Chicken Tenders

1 1/2 pounds boneless, skinless chicken breast halves, cut into small strips

1 tablespoon canola oil

3/4 teaspoon salt

1/2 teaspoon ground black pepper

1/2 cup hot pepper sauce (Frank's Original is preferred)

1 tablespoon butter, melted

1 tablespoon Worcestershire sauce

1/2 teaspoon garlic powder

1/2 teaspoon onion powder

For the dip, place the cheese in a medium bowl, and slightly mash it with the back of a fork. Mix in the buttermilk, mayonnaise, mustard, salt, and pepper until the dip is slightly chunky.

Heat the grill to medium-high heat. Toss the chicken strips in a bowl with the oil, salt, and pepper. Place them on the grill, and cook for 2 to 3 minutes per side, until they are cooked through.

While the chicken is grilling, whisk together the hot pepper sauce, butter, Worcestershire sauce, garlic powder, and onion powder in a large bowl. Leaving the grill on, remove the chicken strips, and toss them in the sauce until they are well coated.

Place the chicken strips back on the grill for another 1 to 2 minutes, until the sauce begins to char, and then remove them to a serving platter. Serve them with the Gorgonzola dip.

Makes 6 servings.

Tip: To prepare this at tailgate, make the dip and the buffalo sauce ahead of the time. Keep the dip chilled just until serving.

PIMENTO CHEESE AND PICKLED ONION SLIDERS

Every year in the middle of July, my dad requests grilled cheeseburgers for his birthday dinner. He has also always loved a good pimento cheese sandwich. So in honor of his two favorite sandwiches, I came up with these grilled pimento cheese mini burgers, also known as sliders. This is a fantastic and simple way to jazz up grilled hamburgers at your next cookout.

PICKLED ONIONS

1/2 cup cider vinegar

1 1/2 tablespoons sugar

1 1/2 teaspoons salt

1 red onion, thinly sliced

PIMENTO CHEESE SLIDERS

1 cup freshly shredded sharp Cheddar cheese

1 tablespoon diced pimentos

3 tablespoons mayonnaise

1 tablespoon plus 1 teaspoon Worcestershire sauce, divided

1 pound ground chuck

3/4 teaspoon salt

3/4 teaspoon ground black pepper

8 small dinner rolls

For the onions, in a small bowl whisk together the vinegar, sugar, and salt. Place the onions in a bowl, and pour the vinegar mixture over the top. Let the onions stand at room temperature for at least 1 hour before using or refrigerate overnight.

For the sliders, in a bowl mix together the cheese, pimentos, mayonnaise, and 1 teaspoon of the Worcestershire sauce. Refrigerate until you are ready to serve the burgers. Form 8 small patties out of the chuck, and season them with salt and pepper. Sprinkle the remaining 1 tablespoon Worcestershire sauce over the patties.

Heat the grill to medium-high heat. Grill the patties for 2 to 3 minutes per side. Reduce the grill heat to low, and spread a spoonful of pimento cheese over each patty. Place the rolls on the grill, and close the lid. Cook for 1 to 2 minutes, until the cheese melts and the rolls are heated.

To serve, split the rolls, and place the mini burgers on the roll bottoms. Top with the pickled onions and roll tops.

MAKES 8 SERVINGS.

STEAK WITH ROASTED GARLIC CHIVE BUTTER

Every now and then there is just nothing that will hit the spot except for a hearty, tender steak. And it only gets better with this roasted garlic and chive butter. This is definitely a dish to impress.

1 whole garlic head

2 teaspoons extra-virgin olive oil

1/4 cup butter, softened

1 1/4 teaspoons salt, divided

1 1/4 teaspoons ground black pepper, divided

1 tablespoon finely chopped chives

3 teaspoons finely grated lemon peel

4 (8-ounce) steaks (rib-eye, sirloin, or strip)

Preheat the oven to 375 degrees. Cut the top quarter of the garlic head off, exposing the individual garlic cloves. Drizzle the olive oil over the cloves, and wrap the garlic in aluminum foil. Place it in the oven, and bake for 40 to 45 minutes, until the cloves are golden and soft. Squeeze the soft garlic out of the bulb into a medium bowl. Add the butter, 1/4 teaspoon of the salt, and 1/4 teaspoon of the pepper, and mash together with a fork until smooth. Stir in the chives. Place the butter mixture on a piece of plastic wrap, and wrap it tightly into a log shape. Refrigerate until time to serve the steaks.

Heat the grill to medium-high heat. Season the steaks on both sides with the remaining 1 teaspoon salt, the remaining 1 teaspoon pepper, and the lemon peel. Place the steaks on the grill, and cook for 6 to 8 minutes per side for medium rare. Remove the steaks from the grill, and let them stand, covered, for 5 minutes. Meanwhile, cut the chilled butter into 4 "coins," and place one on each steak before serving immediately.

MAKES 4 SERVINGS.

Smoky Sweet Pulled Pork

Barbecue sandwiches are without a doubt the go-to main dish for Southern events throughout the year, but especially for outdoor summer gatherings. We love our pulled pork, and depending on where you are, you'll come across different styles and methods of preparing it. Since most people don't have a smoker, this pulled pork is prepared in a slow cooker, and it calls for a secret ingredient to achieve that heavenly smoky flavor.

Spice Rub

1 tablespoon brown sugar

2 teaspoons chili powder

2 teaspoons ground cumin

2 teaspoons paprika

2 teaspoons salt

2 teaspoons ground black pepper

1 teaspoon garlic powder

1 teaspoon onion powder

1/2 teaspoon ground cinnamon

Pork Barbecue

1 (3- to 4-pound) trimmed pork shoulder

1 cup root beer

2 tablespoons liquid smoke

Barbecue Sauce

1 tablespoon butter

1/2 cup chopped white onion

1 cup ketchup

1/3 cup cider vinegar

1/3 cup firmly packed brown sugar

2 tablespoons prepared yellow mustard

1 tablespoon liquid smoke

1/4 teaspoon salt

1/2 teaspoon ground black pepper

For the spice rub, in a small bowl stir together the brown sugar, chili powder, cumin, paprika, salt, pepper, garlic powder, onion powder, and cinnamon.

For the pork, rub the spice rub all over the meat. Place the meat in a slow cooker, and pour in the root beer and liquid smoke. Cook on low for 7 to 8 hours.

For the barbecue sauce, melt the butter in a saucepan over medium heat, and then add the onions. Cook the onions until they are softened, for 2 to 3 minutes. Stir in the ketchup, vinegar, brown sugar, mustard, liquid smoke, salt, and pepper. Cook for another 5 to 6 minutes.

When the pork is done, remove it from the slow cooker, and pull it apart using two forks. Remove most of the liquid from the slow cooker, leaving only about 1 cup, and return the pulled pork to the cooker. Add the prepared barbecue sauce as well. Stir everything together, cover, and cook on low for another 30 minutes. Keep the slow cooker on warm while serving.

Makes 10 to 12 servings.

Brown Sugar Bacon Club Sandwiches

A few special touches take this club sandwich from ordinary to extraordinary.
Seriously, could anything be better than brown sugar and bacon?

¹/₃ cup brown sugar	¹/₄ teaspoon ground black pepper
8 uncooked bacon slices	12 slices white or wheat bread, lightly toasted
¹/₂ cup mayonnaise	16 turkey slices
2 tablespoons fresh lemon juice	8 romaine lettuce leaves
¹/₄ teaspoon salt	8 tomato slices

Preheat the oven to 400 degrees. Line a baking sheet with a wire rack. Place the brown sugar in a shallow bowl. Dredge each piece of bacon in the sugar on each side, and then place them on the rack. Bake for about 20 minutes or until the bacon is crisp. Break each slice in half.

In a small bowl whisk together the mayonnaise, lemon juice, salt, and pepper. Spread the mayo mixture on 4 slices of the bread. Top those slices with 2 slices of turkey, 2 bacon halves, one lettuce leaf, and one tomato slice. Spread mayo on one side of 4 more slices of bread and place on top of the tomato. Repeat the layers. Spread the mayonnaise on the last 4 slices of bread, and top all the sandwiches with the mayo side down. Cut the sandwiches diagonally into quarters, securing each triangle with a long toothpick or cocktail sword.

Makes 4 servings.

TIP: Wrap these sandwiches in parchment paper to maintain freshness when transporting.

PEPPERED STEAK SANDWICHES

This is certainly a man's sandwich, and a delicious option for celebrating the man of the family's birthday. The sweet, grilled red onion balances out the pepper-rubbed steak and horseradish just enough.

HORSERADISH SAUCE

1/3 cup mayonnaise

2 teaspoons prepared horseradish

2 teaspoons Dijon mustard

1/8 teaspoon salt

STEAK SANDWICHES

2 teaspoons coarsely ground black pepper

1/2 teaspoon white pepper

1 teaspoon salt

4 (6-ounce) sirloin steaks

1 red onion

4 ciabatta rolls

For the sauce, mix together the mayonnaise, horseradish, mustard, and salt in a small bowl. Refrigerate until you are ready to assemble the sandwiches.

For the sandwiches, mix together the black pepper, white pepper, and salt in a small bowl. Rub the spice mixture evenly onto both sides of the steaks. Let them stand for at least 20 minutes. Slice the onion into 1/4-inch rounds.

Heat the grill to medium-high heat. Place the steak on the grill directly over the heat, and grill it for 6 minutes per side for medium. After flipping the steaks, place the onions on the grill, and cook them for 2 to 3 minutes per side. Remove the steak and onions, and cover them with aluminum foil.

Split the rolls, and spread the horseradish mayonnaise on the inside of each half. Thinly slice the steaks against the grain, and pile the meat onto the roll bottoms, followed by the onions and the tops of the rolls. Serve the sandwiches warm or at room temperature.

MAKES 4 SERVINGS.

Broadway Under the Stars

JACK LONDON STATE HISTORIC PARK
Glen Ellen, California
June through September
Transcendencetheater.org

Broadway Under the Stars is a series of award-winning concerts featuring established Broadway and Hollywood performers in the majestic open-air winery ruins at the Jack London State Historic Park in beautiful Sonoma County, California.

Each evening begins with picnicking on the great lawn alongside the park's sprawling vineyards, where, as you would expect, you'll enjoy local pours from numerous Sonoma wineries as well as preshow music.

Broadway Under the Stars weaves your favorite Broadway and popular songs into a spectacular evening that will leave you wanting more. And that is just what a good night of food and music is supposed to do.

HARVEST TURKEY BURGERS

*The grated apple in these autumn-themed turkey burgers adds a hint of
sweetness and keeps them moist. I prefer to use ground turkey that includes the
white and dark meat for these burgers so they don't dry out on the grill.*

1 tablespoon maple syrup	2 teaspoons Worcestershire sauce
1 tablespoon Dijon mustard	1/2 teaspoon salt
6 slices bacon	1/2 teaspoon garlic powder
1 apple	1/2 teaspoon dry mustard
1 pound ground turkey, white and dark meat	6 slices sharp Cheddar cheese
1/4 cup sliced green onions	6 hamburger buns

Preheat the oven to 400 degrees. Mix together the maple syrup and Dijon mustard in a small bowl. Place a wire rack on top of a baking sheet. Coat each strip of bacon with the maple mixture on each side, and place on the wire rack. Bake for 15 minutes, or until the bacon is crisp.

Grate the apple, and then squeeze out the excess juice. In a large bowl combine the turkey, grated apple, green onions, Worcestershire sauce, salt, garlic powder, and dry mustard. Be careful not to over mix the ingredients. Form the turkey mixture into 6 patties, and refrigerate until you are ready to grill.

Heat the grill to medium-high heat. Place the burgers on the grill, and cook for 4 to 5 minutes on each side. Place the cheese on the burgers for the last minute of grilling. Break each strip of cooked bacon into halves, and place 2 half strips on each cooked burger. Place the burgers on the buns and serve warm.

MAKES 6 SERVINGS.

Sizzlin' Cowboy Chili

This chili recipe is hearty, rich, and sure to warm you up from the inside on a crisp fall day. I like to make this on the stovetop and then transfer it to a slow cooker to keep it warm for transporting to the big game.

2 teaspoons salt, divided

1 teaspoon ground black pepper, divided

2 pounds cubed stew meat

2 tablespoons canola oil

2 medium white onions, chopped

2 medium jalapeño peppers, seeds removed and finely chopped

2 (6-ounce) cans tomato paste

4 cloves garlic, finely chopped

2 teaspoons chili powder

2 teaspoons ground cumin

1 teaspoon paprika

8 cups low-sodium beef broth

2 (16-ounce) cans red kidney beans, drained and rinsed

Sprinkle 1 teaspoon of the salt and 1/2 teaspoon of the pepper all over the stew meat. Place the oil in a Dutch oven or large pot, and heat over medium-high heat. Add the meat, cook for 2 minutes per side side, and then remove the meat from the pot.

Add the onions and jalapeños to the drippings, and cook over medium heat until the onions begin to soften, for 7 to 8 minutes, stirring occasionally. Add the tomato paste, garlic, chili powder, cumin, and paprika. Cook for another 2 to 3 minutes, stirring often. Stir in the broth, the remaining 1 teaspoon salt,

and the remaining 1/2 teaspoon black pepper. Return the meat to the pot, and bring the mixture to a boil. Reduce the heat to low, and simmer, uncovered, for 1 1/2 hours. Add the beans to the chili, cover, and cook until the beats are heated through. Transfer the chili to a slow cooker to keep it warm or serve from the stovetop.

MAKES 6 TO 8 SERVINGS.

GRILLED BARBECUE CHICKEN PIZZA

If I let him, I believe my husband would have pizza every night of his life. It's his absolute favorite food. So when I make this barbecue chicken pizza for him, he is in hog heaven. If you have never tried grilling pizza, it's really a treat and so simple. Once you try it, I guarantee you'll be hooked.

1 tablespoon butter

3/4 cup chopped red onion

1 pound pizza dough (prepared from a package or purchased at a deli)

Canola oil for the grill

1/3 cup prepared barbecue sauce

1 cup chopped, cooked chicken breast

3 slices bacon, cooked and crumbled

1/4 cup crumbled blue cheese

1/2 cup freshly shredded Cheddar cheese

2 tablespoons chopped cilantro

Melt the butter in a skillet over low heat. Add the onions, and cook them, stirring occasionally, until golden, for about 20 minutes.

Heat the grill to medium-high heat. Roll out the pizza dough to about 12 inches in diameter. Dip a paper towel in the oil, and use tongs to rub the towel over the grill grates. Place the rolled-out dough on the grill, and cook for 2 minutes, or until it is charred on one side. Transfer the dough from the grill to a baking sheet, grilled side up.

Spread the grilled side of the dough evenly with the barbecue sauce. Evenly distribute the onions, chicken, bacon, blue cheese, and Cheddar cheese over the top. Place the pizza back on the grill, and close the lid. Cook for 2 to 3 minutes, until the cheese is melted and the bottom side is charred. Remove the pizza from the grill. Sprinkle the top with the cilantro. Slice and serve warm.

MAKES 4 SERVINGS.

Sunshine Citrus Chicken

I call this one "sunshine" chicken because of the bright flavors used in the marinade. This is one of my go-to recipes when it comes to grilled chicken in the summer. Chicken thighs are my absolute favorite part of the chicken because they are so delightfully moist, and even if you happen to overcook them, they don't dry out easily.

2 pounds boneless chicken thighs

1 teaspoon finely grated orange peel

1 cup fresh orange juice

1/2 teaspoon finely grated lemon peel

1/4 cup fresh lemon juice

1/2 teaspoon finely grated lime peel

2 tablespoons fresh lime juice

1/2 cup canola oil

3 cloves garlic, finely chopped

1/2 cup sliced green onions

1 tablespoon honey

1 1/2 teaspoons salt

1 teaspoon ground black pepper

Place the chicken thighs in a large ziptop bag. In a small bowl stir together the orange peel and juice, lemon peel and juice, lime peel and juice, oil, garlic, green onions, honey, salt, and pepper. Pour the mixture over the chicken thighs. Seal the bag, and place in the refrigerator to marinate for at least 2 hours or overnight.

Heat the grill to medium-high heat.

Remove the chicken from the marinade, and discard marinade. Place the chicken thighs on the grill, and cook them for 7 to 8 minutes per side. Serve the chicken warm off the grill.

MAKES 6 SERVINGS.

SMOKED GOUDA ROAST BEEF SANDWICHES

These tasty roast beef sandwiches are perfect for making ahead and heating up on the grill or serving chilled at a picnic. The sundried tomato pesto adds a tangy flavor to the rich roast beef.

1/2 cup sundried tomatoes in oil, drained and chopped

1 clove garlic, roughly chopped

1/4 cup fresh basil leaves

1/4 cup freshly grated Parmesan cheese

1/3 cup extra-virgin olive oil

12 ounces thinly sliced roast beef

4 hamburger buns

4 slices smoked Gouda cheese

Place the sundried tomatoes, garlic, basil, and Parmesan in the bowl of a food processor, and pulse until ingredients are finely ground. Slowly drizzle in the oil through the chute with the motor running.

Layer the roast beef evenly on the bottom buns, top with the Gouda, and spread the inside of the top of the buns with the sundried tomato mixture. Top the sandwiches, and then wrap each individually in aluminum foil. The sandwiches may be eaten cold or heated on a grill over indirect heat for about 10 minutes for a roast beef melt.

MAKES 4 SERVINGS.

LEAN, MEAN PINTO BEAN BURGER

As much as I love a hearty hamburger, occasionally I must cater to a non-meat eater. To my surprise, these hearty pinto bean burgers were a hit, even with the men in my family. You can top them with the regular hamburger fixings, but I prefer some chunky salsa on these instead of ketchup.

1 (16-ounce) can pinto beans, drained and rinsed

$1/2$ cup cooked brown rice

$1/2$ cup chopped roasted red bell pepper

$1/4$ cup sliced green onions

1 clove garlic, finely chopped

1 large egg, lightly beaten

$1/3$ cup dry bread crumbs

$1/2$ teaspoon ground cumin

$3/4$ teaspoon salt

$1/2$ teaspoon ground black pepper

1 tablespoon canola oil

Colby cheese slices and salsa, for topping

Pour the beans into a medium bowl. Using a potato masher or the back of a fork, mash the beans until they are slightly chunky. Mix in the rice, red peppers, green onions, and garlic. Add the egg, bread crumbs, cumin, salt, and pepper. Stir until well combined. Form 4 patties out of the mixture, and place them on squares of waxed or parchment paper. Refrigerate the patties for at least 30 minutes before grilling them.

Heat the grill to medium-high heat. Lightly brush the burgers with the oil. Place the burgers on the grill, and cook them for 4 to 5 minutes per side. Top with the cheese and salsa if desired, and serve warm off the grill.

MAKES 4 SERVINGS.

TENNESSEE FISH TACOS WITH CREAMY JALAPEÑO SLAW

I call these "Tennessee tacos" because you probably won't find fresh catfish tacos anywhere by the beach. Our ponds and lakes in Tennessee are full of good catfish, usually perfect for frying but also for grilled tacos.

JALAPEÑO SLAW

3 cups thinly sliced green cabbage

3 cups thinly sliced purple cabbage

1/2 cup sour cream

1/4 cup mayonnaise

2 tablespoons fresh lime juice

1 tablespoon finely chopped jalapeño pepper

2 tablespoons sliced green onions

1/4 teaspoon salt

FISH TACOS

1/4 teaspoon chipotle chili powder

1/2 teaspoon paprika

1/2 teaspoon ground cumin

1/2 teaspoon salt

1 1/2 pounds catfish filets

Flour tortillas

For the slaw, place the green and purple cabbage in a large bowl. In a small bowl mix together the sour cream, mayonnaise, lime juice, jalapeños, green onions, and salt. Pour the dressing over the cabbage, and toss to coat the cabbage completely. Refrigerate the slaw until you are ready to serve.

For the fish tacos, mix together the chili powder, paprika, cumin, and salt in a bowl. Sprinkle the spice mixture all over the catfish filets.

Heat the grill to medium-high heat. Grill the fish for 3 minutes per side, or until it is flaky. Meanwhile, wrap the tortillas in aluminum foil, and place them on the grill to heat. Remove the fish and tortillas from the grill, and use two forks to flake the fish apart. Assemble the tacos and top them with the slaw.

MAKES 4 TO 6 SERVINGS.

TIP: Be sure your grill is very clean and oiled before grilling this delicate fish.

PICNIC FRIED CHICKEN DRUMSTICKS

What kind of Southerner would I be if I didn't include a classic fried chicken recipe in this cookbook? This recipe gets an extra-crunchy coating so these chicken legs will stay nice and crisp even at a picnic.

12 chicken legs

2 tablespoons hot pepper sauce

3 cups buttermilk

1 cup all-purpose flour

2 large eggs, beaten

2 cups crushed cornflakes

2 teaspoons Cajun seasoning

1 teaspoon salt

1 teaspoon ground black pepper

Peanut oil, for frying

Cooking spray

Place the chicken legs in a large ziptop bag or large container. Pour the hot pepper sauce and buttermilk into the bag. Seal the bag, and refrigerate for at least 2 hours or overnight.

Place the flour in a shallow dish and the eggs in another shallow dish. In a third shallow dish stir together the corn flakes, Cajun seasoning, salt, and pepper.

Preheat the oven to 350 degrees, and heat the peanut oil in a heavy pot to 350 degrees. Place a wire rack over a large baking sheet, and spray the rack with cooking spray.

Remove the chicken legs from the buttermilk. Roll each one in the flour, and then the egg, and then the cornflake mixture. Fry the chicken in three batches for 3 to 4 minutes per side. Place the fried chicken on the rack, and bake it for 20 minutes.

MAKES 6 SERVINGS.

TIP: Frying the chicken in batches keeps the oil from cooling down too much.

DELTA CLASSIC CHASTAIN PARK

ATLANTA, GEORGIA
MAY THROUGH OCTOBER
WWW.CLASSICCHASTAIN.COM

What better way to unwind with friends and family than at a concert under the stars at Atlanta's own Delta Classic Chastain Park? This seven-thousand-seat amphitheater is situated among gorgeous oak and magnolia trees, making for a delightful space for al fresco dining and amazing performances.

Since 1973, this outdoor facility has featured unforgettable musicians—from "the Godfather of Soul" James Brown to distinguished country music artists such as Martina McBride. On occasion, the Atlanta Symphony Orchestra accompanies the performers for a truly grand concert experience.

The shows run from May to October each year, but make sure you buy your tickets in advance. Bring a blanket to enjoy a meal on the grounds, or dress up a picnic table for a special celebration feast. Whether it's a romantic date for two or a night to visit with friends, this is a fantastic venue for everyone to enjoy a wonderful show and meal in the open air.

Blackberry-Lime Glazed Pork Tenderloin

*I didn't grow up eating pork tenderloin, but once I discovered it, I was in love.
It's a lean meat that is still really tender. This one gets an extra kick from
the spice rub and a rich sweetness from the blackberry glaze.*

Rub and Pork

1/2 teaspoon ground cumin

1/2 teaspoon chili powder

1/2 teaspoon paprika

1/2 teaspoon ground black pepper

1 teaspoon sugar

1 1/4 teaspoons salt

2 (1-pound) pork tenderloins

Blackberry-Lime Glaze

1 tablespoon canola oil

1 shallot, finely chopped

1 clove garlic, finely chopped

1/2 cup blackberry jam

1 teaspoon finely grated lime peel

1 tablespoon fresh lime juice

1 tablespoon Dijon mustard

1 tablespoon red wine vinegar

1/4 teaspoon salt

1/4 teaspoon ground black pepper

For the rub, in a small bowl stir together the cumin, chili powder, paprika, pepper, sugar, and salt. Rub the spice mixture all over the pork tenderloins.

For the glaze, heat the oil in a saucepan over medium heat. Add the shallots and garlic, and cook them until they are softened. Stir in the jam, lime peel and juice, mustard, vinegar, salt, and pepper. Increase the heat to medium-high, and cook until the jam is reduced and slightly thickened, for 6 to 8 minutes.

Heat the grill to medium-high heat. Place the pork over direct heat, and cook it for 10 to 12 minutes, rotating every 3 to 4 minutes, until the outside of the pork is charred. Brush the pork with the glaze while continuing to cook for another 5 to 6 minutes, rotating it every couple of minutes to keep the pork from burning. Remove the pork from the grill, cover it with aluminum foil, and let it rest for 5 minutes before slicing. Serve the pork with any remaining glaze drizzled on top.

Makes 6 servings.

Maple Grilled Salmon

If you are intimidated by the thought of grilling fish, don't be. The key is to make sure your grill is clean and lightly oiled before grilling to help prevent any sticking.

2 tablespoons cider vinegar

2 tablespoons maple syrup

1 tablespoon canola oil

2 teaspoons spicy brown mustard

2 teaspoons finely chopped, peeled fresh
   ginger

1 teaspoon liquid smoke

1/2 teaspoon salt

1/2 teaspoon ground black pepper

4 (6-ounce) skin-on salmon fillets

Mix together the vinegar, maple syrup, oil, mustard, ginger, liquid smoke, salt, and pepper in a small bowl. Place the salmon in a large ziptop bag or shallow dish, and pour the marinade over the fish to coat. Seal the bag or cover the dish, and refrigerate the fish for at least 30 minutes or up to 2 hours.

Heat the grill to medium-high heat. Remove the fish from the marinade, and discard the marinade. Place the fish flesh side down on the grill, and cook for 4 to 5 minutes. Using a metal spatula, carefully flip the fish and grill for another 4 minutes. Serve the fish, immediately after grilling.

MAKES 4 SERVINGS.

GRILLED SUMMER VEGGIE SANDWICHES

Marinating the veggies for these sandwiches really takes them to a whole new level. The grilled veggies are so hearty and flavorful that when I serve these sandwiches to my family, they never even miss the meat!

---

4 large portobello mushrooms

2 medium red or yellow bell peppers

2 medium zucchini

1/4 cup fresh lemon juice

1 teaspoon lemon zest

1/4 cup extra-virgin olive oil

2 garlic cloves, minced

2 teaspoons fresh thyme

4 ounces goat cheese

3 tablespoons prepared basil pesto

4 ciabatta rolls, split

Remove the stems from the portabella caps, cut the sides off of the peppers, and cut the zucchini lengthwise into 1/4-inch slices. Place all of the vegetables in a large resealable plastic bag. Add the lemon juice, zest, oil, garlic, and thyme to the bag, and allow the vegetables to marinate for at least 30 minutes or up to 4 hours.

Once the vegetables have marinated, preheat a grill to medium-high heat. Grill the vegetables for 3 to 4 minutes per side until grill marks have formed. While the vegetables are grilling, mix together the goat cheese and pesto in a small bowl. Place the split sides of the rolls on the grill for about 30 seconds just to heat them up. Spread the pesto mixture onto both sides of the ciabatta rolls. Once the vegetables are tender, layer them onto the bread, using the mushroom cap as the base of the sandwich.

MAKES 4 SERVINGS.

TIP: Make these ahead, and serve them chilled or at room temperature for a picnic.

Gorgonzola-Stuffed Burgers with Sweet Onion and Tomato Jam

This burger is stuffed with butter and cheese, so we are off to a pretty good start. But the sweet onion and tomato jam really put this burger over the top. It's the ultimate sweet and tangy burger condiment.

Burgers

3 tablespoons butter, softened

1/2 cup Gorgonzola cheese

1 1/4 pounds ground beef

1 teaspoon salt

1 teaspoon ground black pepper

Hamburger buns

Sweet Onion and Tomato Jam

1 tablespoon olive oil

2 cups sliced Vidalia onion (or sweet yellow onion)

1 (8-ounce) jar sundried tomatoes in oil, chopped and drained

1 1/2 cups water

1/4 cup red wine vinegar

2 tablespoons brown sugar

1/4 teaspoon salt

1/8 teaspoon ground black pepper

For the burgers, stir together the butter and Gorgonzola in a small bowl until they are well combined. Form the mixture into a log, and wrap with plastic wrap. Refrigerate for at least 30 minutes or until firm. Slice the log into 4 sections.

Divide the ground beef into 4 pieces and roll each into a ball. Make a well into the center of each ball, and stuff it with one section of the butter mixture. Mold the beef around the butter mixture, and flatten the beef into patties. Sprinkle both sides of the patties with the salt and pepper. Refrigerate the stuffed patties until you are ready to grill them.

For the jam, heat the oil in a saucepan over low heat, and add the sliced onions. Cook the onions, stirring them occasionally, for 20 minutes. Stir in the sundried tomatoes, water, vinegar, brown sugar, salt, and pepper. Increase the heat to medium-high, and bring the mixture to a boil. Reduce the heat to low, and cook, covered, for 30 minutes. The mixture should have a jam consistency.

Heat the grill to medium-high heat. Place

the burgers on the grill, and cook them for 6 to 7 minutes per side. Place the burgers on the buns, top them with the onions and tomato jam, and serve warm.

Makes 4 servings.

Tip: To serve these at a tailgate, make the patties and the jam ahead of time, and chill them in a cooler until you are ready to grill and assemble the burgers.

Fruity Yogurt Chicken Salad

This is a light and refreshing chicken salad that is delicious scooped over a bed of greens or served on a croissant. The slightly sweet flavor and colorful fruit really set this salad apart from any other chicken salad I have tried.

$1/2$ cup vanilla Greek yogurt

$1/3$ cup light mayonnaise

2 tablespoons fresh lemon juice

$1/2$ teaspoon salt

$1/4$ teaspoon ground black pepper

4 cups chopped, cooked chicken breast

1 cup chopped strawberries

1 cup mandarin oranges

$1/2$ cup sliced almonds

2 green onions, sliced

Whisk together the yogurt, mayonnaise, lemon juice, salt, and pepper in a small bowl. In a large bowl toss together the chicken, strawberries, oranges, almonds, and green onions. Pour the dressing over the chicken mixture, and toss everything together gently until the chicken is well coated and the salad is mixed.

Refrigerate the salad for about 30 minutes before serving it on croissants or on top of mixed greens.

Makes 4 to 6 servings.

CONCERTS IN THE VILLAGE

MATTIE KELLEY CULTURAL ARTS VILLAGE
DESTIN, FLORIDA
THURSDAY NIGHTS IN MAY AND JUNE
WWW.MATTIEKELLYARTSFOUNDATION.ORG

Destin, Florida, has been a summer vacation destination for Southerners for years, not only for its pristine blue waters, but also because it's within driving distance from most Southern states. After a day spent unwinding by the sea, everyone's thoughts turn to food and entertainment for the night. Well, both of those needs are easily met with Concerts in the Village, a nine-week outdoor summer concert series that takes place at Mattie Kelly Cultural Arts Village, right in the heart of Destin. This event, featuring a variety of musical genres including Motown, jazz, and the golden oldies, has been named one of "the top ten things to do" in northwest Florida by *Florida Travel and Tourism Magazine.*

Since picnics are welcome, find a local seafood market and enjoy some of the Gulf's freshest catches in your basket. This is a perfect opportunity to pack a beach-themed picnic with some local shrimp salad and key lime pie. Seating for the concerts is first-come first-served, so shake the sand off those beach chairs and fill that cooler back up for an evening of family entertainment on the Emerald Coast.

Lowcountry Shrimp Boil

A shrimp boil is a great way to feed a crowd while showcasing the freshest shrimp and sweetest summer corn. You might have seen this spread out on a big table covered in newspaper, an easy clean-up trick when serving this classic Lowcountry dish.

Cocktail Sauce

1/2 cup chili sauce

1/2 cup ketchup

1 tablespoon fresh lemon juice

1 teaspoon Worcestershire sauce

2 teaspoons prepared horseradish

Shrimp Boil

4 quarts water

1/2 cup old Bay Seasoning

2 teaspoons salt

4 sprigs fresh thyme

1 large lemon, cut into quarters

2 medium white onions, cut into quarters

4 cloves garlic, crushed

2 pounds red potatoes, cut into halves

2 pounds smoked sausage, cut into 1-inch pieces

6 to 8 ears of corn, cut into halves

3 pounds large unpeeled shrimp

1/2 cup (1 stick) butter

For the cocktail sauce, in a bowl mix together the chili sauce, ketchup, lemon juice, Worcestershire sauce, and horseradish. Refrigerate until you are ready to serve.

For the shrimp boil, bring the water, Old Bay seasoning, salt, thyme, lemons, onions, and garlic to a boil in a large pot over high heat. Add the potatoes, and cook for 6 to 8 minutes. Add the sausage and corn, and cook for another 8 minutes. Add the shrimp, and cook until they are pink, for 2 to 3 more minutes.

Use a large slotted spoon or strainer to transfer the vegetables, sausage, and shrimp to a large serving platter. (Or spread several layers of newspaper on a picnic table, and place them directly on the paper.) Pour several ladles full of the hot cooking liquid over the shrimp boil, and place pats of the butter on top. Serve warm with the cocktail sauce.

Makes 6 to 8 servings.

Marinated Flank Steak with Roasted Cherry Tomatoes

Flank steak is a fantastic way to feed a group of people steak without breaking the bank. It is wonderfully tender when marinated and cooked to medium-rare. The simple roasted tomatoes give this steak a zesty pop of flavor, which really rounds out the dish.

Marinade

1/4 cup canola oil

2 tablespoons lemon juice

2 teaspoons fresh lemon zest

1/3 cup soy sauce

3 garlic cloves, minced

1 tablespoon fresh thyme

1 (2-pound) flank steak

Roasted Tomatoes

4 cups cherry tomatoes

2 tablespoons canola oil

2 tablespoons balsamic vinegar

1/2 teaspoon salt

1/2 teaspoon ground black pepper

2 teaspoons fresh thyme

To make the marinade, in a small bowl whisk together the oil, lemon juice, zest, soy sauce, garlic, and thyme. Place the steak in a dish or large resealable plastic bag. Pour the marinade over the steak, and refrigerate for at least 2 hours or up to overnight.

To make the roasted tomatoes, preheat the oven to 400 degrees. Place the tomatoes on a baking sheet, and toss with the oil, balsamic vinegar, salt, pepper, and thyme. Roast the tomatoes for 10 minutes, toss them, and return to the oven for 10 more minutes.

Preheat the grill to medium-high heat. Place the steak on the grill, and cook 7 to 8 minutes per side for medium. Remove the steak from the grill to a cutting board, and cover with aluminum foil for 5 to 10 minutes. Slice the steak against the grain into ½-inch slices, and transfer to a serving dish. Top with the roasted tomatoes.

Makes 4 servings.

Cherry Cola Smoked Baby Back Ribs

The secret to cooking ribs is to go low and slow, and you can even do this on a gas grill. Each component of this recipe is necessary to have flavorful and tender ribs without a smoker. Be sure to prepare everything ahead of time so that you can simply grill and baste on location.

Dry Rub and Ribs

1/4 cup firmly packed brown sugar

1 tablespoon paprika

1 tablespoon salt

2 teaspoons ground black pepper

2 teaspoons garlic powder

2 teaspoons onion powder

2 teaspoons dry mustard

1 teaspoon ground cumin

1 teaspoon oregano

2 (3-pound) slabs of baby back ribs

Hickory woods chips

Mop Sauce

1/2 cup cider vinegar

1/4 cup canola oil

1/4 cup sugar

Cherry Cola Barbecue Sauce

1 cup cherry cola

1 cup ketchup

2 tablespoons cider vinegar

2 teaspoons Worcestershire sauce

2 tablespoons Dijon mustard

2 teaspoons hot pepper sauce

1/2 teaspoon salt

1/2 teaspoon ground black pepper

For the dry rub, in a bowl mix together the brown sugar, paprika, salt, pepper, garlic powder, onion powder, dry mustard, cumin, and oregano. Rinse the ribs in cold water, and pat them dry with paper towels. Remove the silver skin from the back of the ribs, and then rub the dry rub all over both sides of the ribs. Refrigerate the ribs for at least 1 hour or overnight.

Place the wood chips in a bowl of water about an hour before you plan to start smoking the ribs. Drain them, and place them in an aluminum foil pouch or smoker box. Place the chips directly over one of the burners, close the grill, and heat the burner under the chips to high heat for about 15 minutes to get the smoke going. While the wood chips are smoking, create the mop sauce.

For the mop sauce, whisk together the vinegar, oil, and the sugar in a bowl.

To smoke the ribs, turn the heat down to medium-low, and place the ribs, bone side down, over the burners that are not in use. Close the grill lid, and cook the ribs for 30 minutes before turning them. The internal temperature of the grill should be about 250 degrees. While the ribs are cooking, make the barbecue sauce.

For the barbecue sauce, mix together the cherry cola, ketchup, vinegar, Worcestershire sauce, Dijon mustard, hot pepper sauce, salt, and pepper in a medium saucepan. Place the saucepan over medium-high heat, and bring the mixture to a boil. Reduce the heat to low, and simmer until thickened, for about 10 minutes.

Once the wood chips stop smoking, remove them from the grill. Cook the ribs for 2 1/2 hours, turning and brushing them with the mop sauce every 30 minutes. Brush both sides of the ribs with the Cherry Cola Barbecue Sauce, and then cook 30 minutes longer. Remove the ribs from the grill, and cover with aluminum foil for 10 minutes before slicing them.

MAKES 4 TO 6 SERVINGS.

DRESSED-UP BLTs

*The quality of a BLT sandwich all comes down to its simple ingredients.
Once you master the classic version, give this dressed-up BLT a try.*

1 large avocado

2 tablespoons mayonnaise

1 tablespoon fresh lemon juice

1 teaspoon honey

1/8 teaspoon salt

8 slices sourdough bread

4 romaine lettuce leaves

1 beefsteak tomato, thickly sliced

12 slices bacon, cooked until crisp

6 ounces blue cheese crumbles

Combine the avocado, mayonnaise, lemon juice, honey, and salt in a bowl, and mash together until smooth. Spread the avocado mixture onto each slice of bread. On half of the bread slices layer the romaine, tomato, bacon, and blue cheese. Place the remaining slices of bread on top. Gently press the sandwiches, and cut them into halves.

MAKES 4 SERVINGS.

TIP: To travel with these BLTs, simply wrap them in plastic wrap, and store them in a cooler until you are ready to serve them.

BBQ-Stuffed Sweet Spud

I actually came up with this recipe by accident. I was going to make barbecue-stuffed russet potatoes, but I realized that all I had was sweet potatoes. So I figured I would give it a try anyway. The result was a sweet and savory combo that was fantastic!

4 large sweet potatoes, washed and dried

4 tablespoons butter, melted

2 tablespoons brown sugar

1/2 teaspoon salt

2 cups pulled pork (leftover or already prepared)

1/2 cup bottled barbecue sauce

1/4 cup sliced green onions

1/2 cup freshly shredded Cheddar cheese

Preheat the oven to 375 degrees. Prick holes in the potatoes, and bake them for 45 minutes to 1 hour, until they are tender. Let the potatoes cool, and then cut a slit lengthwise across the tops. Squeeze the bottoms of the potatoes to expose more of the flesh. Evenly pour the melted butter over the potato flesh, and sprinkle with the brown sugar and salt.

Combine the pulled pork, barbecue sauce, and green onions, and toss together until well mixed. Evenly distribute the pork mixture over the potatoes, and then top with the cheese.

Heat the grill to medium heat. Place the potatoes over indirect heat, close the grill lid, and cook them for 15 to 20 minutes, until the cheese has melted and the stuffing is heated through.

Makes 4 servings.

Louisiana State University Tailgating

TIGER STADIUM
Baton Rouge, Louisiana
Fall
WWW.LSUSPORTS.NET

Each corner of the South has its own preferred tailgating cuisine, but at most tailgating venues you'll find the usual suspects: pulled pork, brats, and hamburgers. The game-day fare outside of Tiger Stadium at Louisiana State University, though, is unique, mostly because the food in Louisiana is unlike anywhere else in the country. Cajun and Creole dishes are everywhere under the purple and gold tents, and the generous Tiger fans are always willing to share.

Big pots of jambalaya and fresh seafood gumbo are just a few of the dishes you will see in abundance at an LSU tailgate. You might even run across some deep-fried gator when the Florida State team comes to town. The serious tailgaters set up their tents the night before to secure a spot, and the cooking begins as early as sunup. After a day of food, music, and fun, tailgaters head into the stadium, known as "Death Valley," with full bellies and high spirits.

"Geau Tigers!" Gumbo

This may not seem like a typical outdoor recipe, but it's definitely appropriate on a fall game day at LSU. Make this soup the day before, and then put it in a slow cooker set on warm to keep it ready for serving outdoors.

1/2 cup canola oil

1/2 cup all-purpose flour

1 medium white onion, chopped

1 medium green bell pepper, chopped

3 ribs celery, chopped

3 cloves garlic, finely chopped

2 teaspoons Creole seasoning

1/2 teaspoon salt

1 teaspoon ground black pepper

1 bay leaf

4 cups low-sodium chicken stock

12 ounces andouille, cut into 1-inch pieces

2 cups sliced, frozen okra

1 pound medium shrimp peeled and deveined

Heat the oil over medium heat in a large pot, and then whisk in the flour. Continue cooking and whisking until the mixture is golden brown, for 12 to 15 minutes. Add the onions, green peppers, and celery, and cook until they are softened, for 10 to 12 minutes. Add the garlic, Creole seasoning, salt, pepper, bay leaf, chicken stock, andouille, and okra.

Bring the soup to a boil, reduce the heat to low, and simmer for 1 hour. Add the shrimp, and cook until they turn pink, for 2 to 3 minutes. Serve immediately, or place the gumbo in a slow cooker to take to your destination, and then set the cooker on warm.

MAKES 6 TO 8 SERVINGS.

Bourbon Apple Candied Wings

The name pretty much says it all—these wings are just to die for! This recipe has all of the bases covered, with a little sweet and a little heat, topped off with a kick of bourbon.

2 tablespoons butter

1 cup chopped Vidalia onion

2 tablespoons finely chopped jalapeño pepper

1 cup apple jelly

1/2 cup bourbon

1 tablespoon Worcestershire sauce

4 pounds chicken wingettes

2 tablespoons canola oil

1 1/2 teaspoons salt

1 teaspoon ground black pepper

Melt the butter in a skillet over medium-low heat. Add the onions, and cook until they are softened, for 6 to 8 minutes. Stir in the jalapeños, jelly, bourbon, and Worcestershire sauce. Increase the heat to medium-high, and cook until the mixture is reduced by half, for 10 to 12 minutes. Remove from the heat, and place in a large bowl.

Heat the grill to medium-high heat. Place the chicken wingettes in a large bowl. Add the oil, salt, and pepper, and toss together until the chicken pieces are well coated. Place them on the hot grill, and cook for 10 to 12 minutes on each side. Add the grilled wings to the glaze, and toss until they are well coated. Return the wings to the grill, and cook for 1 to 2 minutes per side, just until the wings are caramelized. Serve them hot off the grill.

MAKES 6 SERVINGS.

MOVIES IN THE PARK

RIVERFRONT PARK
LITTLE ROCK, ARKANSAS
WEDNESDAY, JUNE THROUGH AUGUST
WWW.MOVIESINTHEPARKLR.NET

In the family-friendly town of Little Rock, Arkansas, dinner and a movie takes on a whole new meaning during the summertime. Along the banks of the Arkansas River, on Wednesdays at sundown, folks bring their picnic baskets and spread out their blankets to enjoy classic films at Little Rock's Riverfest Amphitheatre.

Don't expect your typical quiet movie theatre atmosphere. Clapping, booing, and loud laughter fill the air at this outdoor cinema. It's as if you're watching a movie with hundreds of your closest friends. There is this sense of community that is created here that can't be duplicated in a hushed theatre. This is an ideal event for an affordable family night out, or bring on the wine and cheese for a laid-back date night. Little Rock's Movies in the Park proves that sometimes the simplest nights out are the best ones.

Jerk Chicken Wraps with Nectarine Salsa

For your next picnic, hold the ham and cheese sandwiches, and give these tasty jerk chicken wraps a try. The fresh nectarine salsa is the perfect match for the slightly spicy chicken, all wrapped up for easy eating. This is the ideal picnic treat.

Nectarine Salsa

1 cup chopped nectarines

1 cup chopped tomatoes

1 tablespoon finely chopped jalapeño pepper

2 tablespoons chopped fresh cilantro

1 tablespoon fresh lime juice

1/8 teaspoon salt

Chicken Wraps

1 teaspoon salt

1 teaspoon ground cumin

1/2 teaspoon ancho chili powder

1/2 teaspoon ground black pepper

1/4 teaspoon allspice

1 1/4 pounds boneless, skinless chicken breast halves

1/4 cup light mayonnaise

4 sandwich wraps

For the salsa, in a medium bowl combine the nectarines, tomatoes, jalapeños, cilantro, lime juice, and salt, and gently toss the ingredients together. Refrigerate the salsa until you are ready to assemble the wraps.

Heat the grill to medium-high heat. In a small bowl mix together the salt, cumin, chili powder, pepper, and allspice. Sprinkle the chicken evenly with the spice mixture. Place the chicken on the grill, and cook for 5 to 6 minutes per side, depending on the thickness of the chicken. Remove the chicken from the grill, and slice it against the grain into 1/2-inch strips.

Spread 1 tablespoon of mayonnaise onto the center of each wrap. Place the sliced chicken on the mayonnaise, and then top the chicken with the salsa. Fold two sides of the wraps in, and then roll them up tightly like a burrito. Slice the wraps into halves diagonally, and refrigerate them until you are ready to serve them.

Makes 4 servings.

Tip: Once you have assembled the wraps, wrap them tightly in plastic wrap, and then store them in a cooler for easy transporting.

SIMPLE SHRIMP SALAD ROLLS

This is an easy shrimp salad recipe that is not overpowered by too many spices. The recipe really allows the fresh shrimp to shine, which is very important in a seafood salad.

1 pound cooked shrimp, peeled and roughly chopped

1/4 cup finely chopped celery

1/4 cup finely chopped red bell pepper

2 tablespoons finely chopped chives

1/4 cup mayonnaise

1/2 teaspoon finely grated lemon peel

1 tablespoon fresh lemon juice

1/2 teaspoon salt

1/4 teaspoon ground black pepper

1/4 teaspoon smoked paprika

4 soft hot dog buns

Combine the shrimp, celery, red peppers, and chives in a large bowl, and toss until well mixed. Add the mayonnaise, lemon peel, lemon juice, salt, pepper, and paprika. Stir until the shrimp and vegetables are well coated. Refrigerate the salad until you are ready to scoop into the buns for serving.

MAKES 4 SERVINGS.

COMEBACK GRILLED CHICKEN SANDWICHES

If you want to look like a star on the grill with an easy recipe, then this is the dish for you! It's a restaurant-quality sandwich, with a special sauce that is sure to have everyone "coming back" for more.

COMEBACK SAUCE

1/2 cup mayonnaise

2 tablespoons chili sauce

1 tablespoon fresh lemon juice

2 teaspoons Worcestershire sauce

1 teaspoon Dijon mustard

1 teaspoon hot pepper sauce

SANDWICHES

4 (6-ounce) boneless, skinless chicken breast halves

1 teaspoon salt

1 teaspoon paprika

3/4 teaspoon garlic powder

3/4 teaspoon onion powder

1/2 teaspoon ground black pepper

4 slices Swiss cheese

2 tablespoons butter, melted

4 hamburger buns

1/2 cup sauerkraut, drained

Mix together the mayonnaise, chili sauce, lemon juice, Worcestershire sauce, mustard, and hot pepper sauce in a small bowl. Refrigerate until you are ready to assemble the sandwiches.

Heat the grill to medium-high heat. Sprinkle the chicken breasts evenly with the salt, paprika, garlic powder, onion powder, and pepper on both sides. Grill the chicken for 7 to 8 minutes per side. During the last few minutes of cooking, place a slice of cheese on each chicken breast, and let it melt.

Brush the melted butter on the insides of the buns, and place them on the grill for about 1 minute, or until they are lightly charred. Spread the sauce onto the insides of the buns. Remove the chicken breasts from the grill, and place them on the bottoms of the buns. Top the chicken with the sauerkraut and the other bun half. Serve immediately with the remaining Comeback Sauce on the side.

MAKES 4 SERVINGS.

"COUNTRY CATCH OF THE DAY" STEAMED TROUT

One of the things my dad is looking forward to doing with my son when he gets older is taking him fishing for the first time. I used to love going with my dad and then coming home to grill our "catch of the day." Since trout is a delicate fish, steaming it in foil on the grill is a foolproof way to prepare it.

4 (6- to 8-ounce) trout fillets

2 tablespoons extra-virgin olive oil

3/4 teaspoon salt

1/4 teaspoon ground black pepper

1 large shallot, thinly sliced

1 tablespoon fresh thyme

1 lemon, thinly sliced

1/4 cup dry white wine

Heat the grill to medium-high heat. Place each trout fillet in the center of a square of aluminum foil. Drizzle the olive oil evenly over each fillet, and then sprinkle with the salt and pepper. Arrange the sliced shallots and thyme on top of the fillets, and then top each with 2 slices of lemon. Pour a splash of the wine on the top of each fillet. Fold the foil over the fillets to create packets.

Place the packets on the grill, and close the lid. Grill them for 6 to 8 minutes, depending on the size of the fillets. Open the packets, and serve the fish immediately.

MAKES 4 SERVINGS.

FRIDAY NIGHT FISH FRY

Backyard fish fries are a tradition where I come from, so I had to share my favorite fried catfish recipe. If you don't have a portable deep fryer, you can easily prepare your fish indoors according to the recipe below, and keep the fish crisp in the oven until you're ready to serve it. Be sure to fry up a batch of hushpuppies (page 102) as well.

CATFISH

2 large eggs

1 cup whole or low-fat milk

2 pounds catfish fillets (4- to 6-ounces each)

1 1/4 cups cornmeal

2 tablespoons all-purpose flour

1 teaspoon salt

1/2 teaspoon seasoning salt

1 teaspoon dry mustard

3/4 teaspoon ground black pepper

1/4 teaspoon celery seed

Peanut oil, for frying

TARTAR SAUCE

1 cup mayonnaise

1 tablespoon fresh lemon juice

1/2 teaspoon Worcestershire sauce

1 tablespoon sweet pickle relish

2 tablespoons grated white onion

For the catfish, preheat the oven to 250 degrees, and place a wire rack on top of a baking sheet. Whisk together the eggs and milk in a shallow dish, and place the catfish fillets in the mixture to soak for about 10 minutes. In another shallow dish mix together the cornmeal, flour, salt, seasoning salt, mustard, pepper, and celery seed.

Heat the oil to 350 degrees in a cast-iron skillet. Remove the fillets from the milk mixture, and dredge them in the cornmeal mixture until they are well coated. Place the fillets in the oil in several batches, and cook them for about 4 minutes per side. Remove the fillets from the oil, and place on the wire rack. Keep the fish in the warm oven until all of the fillets are fried.

For the tartar sauce, mix together the mayonnaise, lemon juice, Worcestershire sauce, relish, and onions in a medium bowl. Keep the sauce chilled until you are ready to serve it with the catfish.

MAKES 4 TO 6 SERVINGS.

DESSERTS

Banana Split Strawberry Pretzel Salad

Strawberry pretzel salad is a special treat that's always served at Southern picnics and barbecues. The sweet, creamy, and salty combination is seriously addictive. This version has all of the flavors of a banana split, and as my dad says, "I could eat the whole pan!"

2 cups pretzels twists

12 chocolate sandwich cookies

5 tablespoons butter, melted

1 (6-ounce) package black cherry gelatin

1 cup sliced strawberries

1 cup sliced bananas

1 (8-ounce) package cream cheese, softened

3/4 cup sugar

1 (8-ounce) container frozen whipped topping, thawed

Preheat the oven to 350 degrees. Grease a 13 x 9-inch baking dish. Place the pretzels and the cookies in the bowl of a food processor, and process until crushed. Stir together the crushed pretzels and cookies with the melted butter. Press the mixture evenly into the baking dish. Bake for 8 minutes, and then let it cool completely.

Prepare the gelatin in a medium bowl according to the package directions, and refrigerate for 1 hour. Add the strawberries and bananas to the gelatin, and then refrigerate for another hour, until the gelatin is slightly thicken but not completely set. Beat the

cream cheese and sugar in a large bowl with an electric or hand mixer until combined. Fold the whipped topping into the cream cheese mixture until it is well incorporated.

Evenly spread the cream cheese mixture on top of the cooled crust, making sure to seal the edges. Spread the gelatin on top, making sure the fruit is evenly spread out. Refrigerate for at least 2 hours before cutting into squares. Serve chilled.

Makes 10 to 12 servings.

LIVE AT THE GARDEN

MEMPHIS BOTANIC GARDEN
MEMPHIS, TENNESSEE
JUNE THROUGH SEPTEMBER
WWW.MEMPHISBOTANICGARDEN.COM

The ninety-six-acre Memphis Botanical Garden features twenty-three specialty gardens that are sure to spark the interest of any nature lover, but this exquisite garden has also become one of the country's most successful outdoor entertainment venues. Live at the Garden is a summer concert series where world-renowned artists, ranging from Earth, Wind, and Fire to Tony Bennett, have performed.

The area in front of the outdoor stage fills up with 2,500 people seated at tables with white linen cloths, and another 4,000 attendees spread across the rest of the lawn, bringing their own chairs and picnic blankets. Where else can you enjoy a star-studded concert surrounded by beautiful gardens for just $45 on the lawn and $69 for a table? Picnics are allowed, so bring some local barbecue for a Memphis night to remember.

FRESH STRAWBERRY LIMEADE CUPCAKES

It's hard to beat a homemade strawberry cupcake, especially for a Southern summer celebration. Not only do these cupcakes taste divine, but the dainty pale-pink color with hints of green will make your guests smile. The fresh lime flavor adds a nice zing that perfectly complements the fresh strawberry cake.

CUPCAKES

2 3/4 cups cake flour

1 tablespoon baking powder

3/4 teaspoon salt

1 cup canola oil

1 2/3 cups plus 3 tablespoons sugar, divided

6 large egg whites

3/4 cup sour cream

2 teaspoons vanilla extract

2 cups chopped strawberries

1/4 cup fresh lime juice

FROSTING

1 cup butter, softened

5 cups powdered sugar, divided

2/3 cup chopped strawberries

2 teaspoons lime zest

To make the cupcakes, preheat the oven to 350 degrees. Place cupcake liners in 24 muffin cups. Whisk together the flour, baking powder, and salt in a medium bowl. In a large bowl, using a mixer on low speed, beat together the oil and 1 2/3 cups of sugar. Add the egg whites one at a time, mixing after each addition. Stir in the sour cream and vanilla, and then slowly mix in the flour mixture. Add the strawberries, mixing just until they are incorporated and the batter is pale pink. Pour the batter into the cupcake liners, filling each three-fourths full. Bake for 20 minutes.

While the cupcakes are baking, heat the lime juice and the remaining 3 tablespoons sugar in a small saucepan over medium heat, stirring until the sugar is dissolved. Once the cupcakes have finished baking, remove them to a wire rack, and use a toothpick to prick several holes in the tops of the cakes while they are still warm. Spoon the lime syrup over the top of each cupcake, and allow the cupcakes to cool completely.

For the frosting, place the butter in a large bowl, and add 1 cup of powdered sugar. Use a hand mixer to cream the mixture. Add the remaining powdered sugar 1 cup at a time, mixing after each addition. Once all of the sugar has been added, stir in the strawberries and lime zest. Frost the cupcakes once they have cooled.

MAKES 24 SERVINGS.

TIP: Keep these cupcakes in a cooler until you are ready to serve them so that the frosting will stay firm.

PUMPKIN SPICED BANANA PUDDING

Old-fashioned "nanner puddin'" is the quintessential dessert of the South. This version gets a fall makeover, perfect for tailgating, with pumpkin and spicy gingersnaps. Happy fall, y'all!

5 cups whole milk, divided

1/4 cup cornstarch

4 large egg yolks

1 1/2 cups pure pumpkin (not pumpkin pie mix)

2 teaspoons vanilla extract

1 cup firmly packed brown sugar

1/2 teaspoon salt

1 teaspoon ground cinnamon

1 teaspoon ground nutmeg

1 cup heavy cream

1/4 cup white sugar

6 cups gingersnaps

4 medium bananas, cut into 1/4-inch slices

Ground cinnamon, for garnish

In a medium bowl whisk together 1 cup of the milk, the cornstarch, egg yolks, pumpkin, and vanilla. In a large saucepan combine the remaining 4 cups milk, the brown sugar, and salt, and bring to a simmer over medium heat. Remove it from the heat, and slowly whisk in the cornstarch mixture. Place the mixture over medium-low heat. Cook, stirring constantly, until the pudding begins to thicken, for 10 to 15 minutes. Once the pudding thickens enough to coat the back of a spoon, remove it from the heat, and add the cinnamon and nutmeg. Refrigerate for at least 30 minutes.

Using an electric mixer, whip the heavy cream on low speed, and then increase the speed as the cream thickens. Add the sugar once soft peaks have formed, and continue mixing until stiff peaks form.

Layer half of the gingersnaps and bananas on the bottom of a large serving bowl, pour half of the pudding over the bananas, and spread half of the whipped cream on top of the pudding. Repeat the layers once more, ending with the whipped cream. Sprinkle the top with cinnamon, if desired. Cover and refrigerate the pudding until you are ready to serve it.

MAKES 8 TO 10 SERVINGS.

OLD-FASHIONED PECAN PIE BARS

Who can resist the ooey-gooey sweetness of homemade pecan pie? It is, without a doubt, a Southern masterpiece. Most Southerners have their own method of making the pecan filling. Some use corn syrup, and some use brown sugar. I prefer to combine the two, which results in a rich filling with a molasses flavor from the brown sugar smoothed out by the silky, light corn syrup.

CRUST

6 tablespoons butter, softened, plus extra to grease the dish

1/4 cup firmly packed brown sugar

1 cup all-purpose flour

1/8 teaspoon salt

PECAN FILLING

2 large eggs

4 tablespoons butter, melted

1/2 cup firmly packed brown sugar

1/2 cup light corn syrup

2 tablespoons all-purpose flour

1 teaspoon vanilla extract

1/4 teaspoon salt

2 tablespoons orange liqueur (optional)

1 cup chopped pecans

Preheat the oven to 350 degrees, and butter an 8-inch square baking dish. For the crust, place the butter and brown sugar in a medium bowl, and beat with a mixer on medium speed until the mixture is light and fluffy, for about 2 minutes. Add the flour and salt, and continue beating just until the mixture comes together. Press the mixture onto the bottom of the baking dish evenly, and bake for 15 minutes, until it is slightly golden. Let the crust cool on a wire rack for at least 10 minutes.

For the filling, in a medium bowl whisk the eggs until they are foamy. Add the butter, brown sugar, corn syrup, flour, vanilla, salt, and orange liqueur, and whisk until the mixture is well blended. Pour the filling mixture over the crust, and evenly sprinkle the pecans on top. Bake for 25 to 28 minutes, until the filling is set. Let cool completely before cutting into squares.

MAKES 16 SERVINGS.

TANGLEWOOD

LENNOX, MASSACHUSETTS
SUMMER
BSO.ORG

One of the most famous and beautiful music venues in the United States, Tanglewood is located in Lennox and Stockbridge, Massachusetts. While is it the summer home to the Boston Symphony Orchestra, Tanglewood also hosts other concerts in many different genres of music including jazz, choral, Broadway, and pop.

While it's a well-known destination venue for many throughout New England, Tanglewood attracts music lovers from all over the world. The Koussevitzky Music Shed at Tanglewood opened in 1938. The Shed seats more than five thousand people and accommodates about twelve thousand additional listeners on its vast lawns.

Whether you are enjoying a homemade picnic dinner or food you picked up in one of Stockbridge's or Lennox's gourmet shops, this idyllic setting and world-class music provide an evening to remember forever.

MAMA'S FROSTED PEANUT BUTTER BROWNIES

My mom's frosted brownies were always a favorite of mine at family cookouts. They were so moist and rich, and the perfect base for a bowl of homemade ice cream. Peanut butter and chocolate are two of my most favorite things in this world. So naturally I combined the two ingredients to make these fudgy, irresistible brownies.

BROWNIES

1/2 cup (1 stick) butter

1/2 cup smooth peanut butter

1/2 cup firmly packed brown sugar

1/2 cup white sugar

1 large egg

1 teaspoon vanilla extract

1 cup all-purpose flour

1/4 teaspoon salt

1/2 teaspoon baking powder

CHOCOLATE GANACHE

3 tablespoons heavy cream

1 cup chopped dark chocolate bar

1/2 teaspoon sea salt

For the brownies, preheat the oven to 350 degrees. Melt the butter in a large saucepan over medium-low heat. Stir in the peanut butter, brown sugar, and white sugar until they are well combined. Remove the saucepan from the heat.

Stir in the egg and vanilla, and mix well. Add the flour, salt, and baking powder, and stir until just combined. Pour the batter in an 8-inch square baking dish, and bake the brownies for 30 to 32 minutes. Remove from the oven, and let the brownies cool completely on a wire rack.

For the ganache, place the cream in a microwave-safe bowl, and microwave for 1 minute. Place the chopped chocolate in a bowl. Pour the hot cream over the chocolate, and whisk until the chocolate is melted.

Spread the ganache over the cooled brownies, and sprinkle with sea salt. Cut into squares, and serve.

MAKES 16 SERVINGS.

Candied Ginger Molasses Cookies

Ginger and molasses are a match made in heaven. These slightly spicy and chewy cookies are always a hit at fall tailgates.

2 cups plus 2 tablespoons all-purpose flour

1/2 teaspoon ground cinnamon

3/4 teaspoon ground ginger

3/4 teaspoon allspice

1/2 teaspoon salt

1 1/2 teaspoons baking soda

1/2 cup (1 stick) butter, softened

1 cup firmly packed brown sugar

1 large egg

1/3 cup molasses

1/4 cup chopped candied ginger

1/3 cup white sugar

In a medium bowl whisk together the flour, cinnamon, ginger, allspice, salt, and baking soda. In a large bowl beat the butter and brown sugar using an electric mixer on medium speed for 2 minutes. Add the egg and molasses to the butter mixture, and continue mixing until the ingredients are well blended. Mix the flour mixture into the butter mixture in two batches, and then stir in the candied ginger until it is well incorporated. Wrap the dough in plastic wrap, and refrigerate for at least 2 hours or overnight.

Preheat the oven to 375 degrees. Line a baking sheet with parchment paper or a silicone baking mat. Place the white sugar in a bowl. Roll the chilled dough into 1-inch balls, and then roll the balls in the white sugar. Place the balls on the baking sheet, and lightly press each cookie with the bottom of a glass. Be sure to space the cookies 2 inches apart. Bake for 8 to 10 minutes. The cookies will be soft. Let them cool for 5 minutes on the baking sheet, and then move them to a wire rack to cool completely.

MAKES 24 COOKIES.

RED RASPBERRY AND GOAT CHEESE ICE CREAM

This ice cream is made the old-fashioned way, which takes a little extra time, but trust me, it is completely worth the effort. The goat cheese is my little tangy secret, which also helps give the ice cream a luscious, creamy texture. This ice cream pairs perfectly with my Lemony White Chocolate Chip Cookies (page 252) for delicious ice-cream sandwiches.

3/4 cup plus 2 tablespoons sugar, divided

6 large egg yolks

2 1/4 cups half-and-half

3 ounces goat cheese, softened

1/4 teaspoon salt

1 teaspoon vanilla extract

6 ounces raspberries

In a large glass bowl whisk together 3/4 cup of the sugar and the egg yolks until the mixture becomes pale yellow and light in texture. Pour the half-and-half into a medium saucepan, and heat it over medium heat until it begins to foam on the edges. Remove the pan from the heat, and slowly pour the hot half-and-half into the egg yolk mixture while whisking constantly.

Place the glass bowl over a saucepan with 2 inches of simmering water, and add the goat cheese. Cook and stir the custard until it thickens and coats the back of a spoon, for 12 to 15 minutes. Remove the bowl from the pan, and add the salt and vanilla.

Let the custard cool to room temperature. Cover it with plastic wrap, allowing the wrap to touch the custard to keep a film from forming, and place it in the refrigerator until it's completely chilled. Pour the chilled custard into a 1 1/2-quart ice-cream freezer, and freeze according to the manufacturer's directions.

Lightly mash together the raspberries and the remaining 2 tablespoons sugar. Once the ice cream is the consistency of soft serve, swirl in the raspberry mixture, being careful not to overmix it. Transfer the ice cream to a freezer-safe container, and freeze for 2 to 3 hours before serving.

MAKES 6 SERVINGS.

LIME SURPRISE BARS

My dad's mother and I share three very special bonds. We absolutely love hot weather, the beach, and last but not least, sweets! There is one dessert that can't be beat on a hot day at the beach: key lime pie. Since I love anything in bar form, I took some of the classic flavors of key lime pie and added a surprise ingredient to make these "to die for" sweet and tart lime bars.

8 (5 x 2-inch) honey graham cracker sheets

3 tablespoons brown sugar

4 tablespoons butter, melted

$1/4$ teaspoon salt

1 (8-ounce) package cream cheese, softened

$1/2$ cup white sugar

1 large egg

1 large egg yolk

1 teaspoon finely grated lime peel

$1/4$ cup fresh lime juice

$1/2$ teaspoon vanilla extract

$1/2$ cup white chocolate chips

Preheat the oven to 350 degrees. Place the graham crackers in the bowl of a food processor or ziptop bag, and pulse or crush them in the bag until fine crumbs are formed. Pour the crumbs into a medium bowl. Add the brown sugar and melted butter, and stir together until the crumbs are moist. Press the crumbs into an 8-inch square baking dish. Bake the crust for 10 minutes, and then let it cool completely.

In a large bowl beat together the cream cheese and white sugar with an electric mixer on medium speed until it is light and fluffy.

Beat in the egg and egg yolk until they are well blended. Mix in the lime peel, lime juice, and vanilla.

Place the white chocolate chips in an even layer on top of the crust. Pour the cream cheese mixture on top, spreading it evenly with a spatula if needed. Bake for 26 to 28 minutes. Let cool completely, and then refrigerate until you are ready to slice and serve.

MAKES 9 SERVINGS.

LEMONY WHITE CHOCOLATE CHIP COOKIES

The first time I tried this combination in a cookie it was at a sub shop, of all places. As soon as I tasted it, I knew I had to get to work coming up with my own version of the recipe. Butter, lemon, and white chocolate all in one a cookie—how could this be bad?

1 cup (2 sticks) butter, softened

1 1/2 cups sugar

2 large eggs

2 1/2 cups all-purpose flour

1 teaspoon salt

1 teaspoon baking powder

1 teaspoon baking soda

3 teaspoons finely grated lemon peel

1/4 cup fresh lemon juice

1 (12-ounce) bag white chocolate chips

Preheat the oven to 350 degrees. Combine the butter and sugar in a large bowl. Using an electric mixer on medium speed, beat the butter and sugar for 2 minutes. Add the eggs, one at a time.

Whisk together the flour, salt, baking powder, and baking soda in a medium bowl. Gradually add the flour mixture to the butter mixture. Mix in the lemon peel and juice. Stir in the white chocolate chips. Refrigerate the dough for 30 minutes. Drop the dough by tablespoonsful 2 inches apart onto a baking sheet, and bake for 12 to 14 minutes. Transfer the cookies to a wire rack, and let them cool completely.

MAKES 30 COOKIES.

PEPSI POPS

OLD TRACE PARK
RIDGELAND, MISSISSIPPI
MAY
WWW.MSORCHESTRA.COM

Every May in Ridgeland, Mississippi, the Mississippi Orchestra kicks off the summer with the annual Pepsi Pops on the Reservoir concert. The event brings in several thousand people, and it's held at Old Trace Park, or "the Rez," as it's known locally. The gates open at 4:30 p.m. with a variety of children's activities and several pre-concert acts on the main stage, followed by the symphonic pops concert presented by the Mississippi Orchestra.

Not only is this a wonderful time for music lovers, it's also a fun event for serious picnickers. Even though there are food vendors at this concert, most attendees bring their own dinners. Some even compete in the annual picnic competition, which is judged on the best picnic design. You can expect to see a wide variety of picnic spreads ranging from simple sandwiches and chips to gourmet fare and themed dinners served on fine china. Regardless of your picnic style, you'll be thrilled by the magnificent finale—a fireworks show after the sun sets, illuminating the sailboats over the water.

Ooey-Gooey S'more Bars

These bars have all of your favorite s'more ingredients baked into one ooey-gooey bar. Kids and adults will love this rich, chewy, and chocolaty dessert that's a snap to make!

---

12 (5 x 2-inch) honey graham cracker sheets

6 tablespoons butter, melted

1/4 teaspoon salt

1 cup semisweet chocolate chips

1 1/2 cups mini marshmallows

1 cup chopped pecans

1 (14-ounce) can sweetened condensed milk

Preheat the oven to 350 degrees. Grease a 9 x 13-inch baking dish.

Break up the graham crackers, and place them in the bowl of a food processor. Pulse until they are finely ground. Stir together the graham cracker crumbs, melted butter, and salt. Press the mixture into the baking dish. Bake for 8 minutes.

Reduce the temperature to 325 degrees. Evenly spread the chocolate chips, marshmallows, and pecans over the warm crust. Evenly pour the sweetened condensed milk over the top. Bake for 20 minutes, or until the marshmallows are light brown. Let the bars cool completely before cutting them into squares.

MAKES 12 SERVINGS.

Oatmeal Raisin Granola Bars

For a summer day at the park or pool, it's nice to have a tasty treat for the kids to snack on that will tide them over until supper. These tasty granola bars will do just that.

Cooking spray

2 cups old-fashioned oats

1/2 cup finely chopped walnuts

1/4 cup corn syrup

1/4 cup maple syrup

1 teaspoon vanilla extract

1 teaspoon ground cinnamon

1/4 teaspoon salt

1/2 cup mini marshmallows

1/2 cup raisins

Preheat the oven to 300 degrees. Coat a 9-inch square baking dish with cooking spray. Place the oats and walnuts on a large baking sheet, and toast in the oven for 12 minutes. Transfer them to a large bowl.

Add the corn syrup, maple syrup, vanilla, cinnamon, and salt to the oats and nuts. Stir everything together until the nuts and oats are well coated. Stir in the marshmallows and raisins, and pour the mixture into the baking dish. Press the mixture into the dish to form an even layer, and then bake it for 20 minutes. Let the granola bars cool for at least 2 hours on the sheet before cutting them. Store the bars in an airtight container.

Makes 9 servings.

Tip: When pressing the granola before baking, wet your fingers to keep the granola from sticking to your hands.

CHOCOLATE LOVER'S CHOCOLATE CREAM PIE

Growing up, I could always count on my mom's parents to have something with chocolate at their house. One of my grandmother's specialties, and a favorite of mine, was her chocolate cream pie. I jazzed this one up a bit with a no-bake chocolate crust and cocoa whipped cream for the chocoholic in us all.

CHOCOLATE CRUST

20 chocolate sandwich cookies

1/4 cup (1/2 stick) butter, melted

CHOCOLATE FILLING

1/2 cup sugar

1/4 cup cocoa powder

1/4 cup cornstarch

1/4 teaspoon salt

2 1/4 cups whole milk

3/4 cup chopped semisweet chocolate, divided

1 teaspoon vanilla extract

WHIPPED CREAM TOPPING

1 cup heavy cream

1 tablespoon powdered sugar

1 tablespoon cocoa powder

For the crust, place the cookies in the bowl of a food processor, and pulse until crumbs are formed. Add the melted butter to the crumbs, and continue pulsing until the mixture is moist throughout. Press into a 9-inch pie pan, and refrigerate for at least 30 minutes.

For the filling, in a medium saucepan whisk together the sugar, cocoa powder, cornstarch, and salt. Slowly whisk in the milk, and cook over medium heat, stirring constantly, for 12 to 15 minutes. After 15 minutes it should have a pudding consistency. Remove the pan from the heat. Immediately stir in 1/2 cup of the chopped chocolate and the vanilla until the chocolate has melted

completely. Let the filling cool for 10 minutes. Pour the filling into the chilled crust, and refrigerate for at least 1 hour.

For the topping, place the cream in a medium bowl. Using an electric mixer, beat the cream until it is slightly thickened. Add the powdered sugar and cocoa powder. Continue beating until stiff peaks form. Spread the cream over the pie, and garnish it with the remaining 1/4 cup chopped chocolate. Loosely cover, and refrigerate the pie overnight. Keep chilled until you are ready to serve.

MAKES 8 SERVINGS.

SHAKESPEARE IN THE PARK

C. DOUGLAS RAMEY AMPHITHEATRE
LOUISVILLE, KENTUCKY
JUNE THROUGH AUGUST
WWW.KYSHAKESPEARE.COM

When you think of Louisville, Kentucky, you probably think of the Derby or maybe the iconic hot brown sandwich (if you are hungry). What you might not know is that Louisville is actually home to the oldest Shakespeare festival in the country.

Nestled in Old Louisville's Central Park, you will find the C. Douglas Ramey Amphitheater where Shakespearean plays are performed at nightfall every summer. The mission of Kentucky Shakespeare's is to enrich the city and the Old Louisville community. These performances, featuring professional actors from across the country, are open to the public and completely free of charge.

What could be more romantic than packing up a picnic, spreading out a blanket, and watching performances of some of the Bard's greatest works under the stars? But wait—it gets better. Before you get your nest made for the performance, be sure to spend some time exploring this beautiful sixteen-acre park. The grounds are characterized by elaborate walkways and border plantings, all situated right in the heart of the city. Now that's a great idea for a midsummer night's dream.

CREAM CHEESE FROSTED RED VELVET BROWNIES

I couldn't write this cookbook without some form of red velvet cake. This is my version in brownie form. But don't worry. I kept everyone's favorite part of the cake—the cream cheese frosting, of course!

RED VELVET BROWNIES

Cooking spray

1/2 cup canola oil

1 cup white sugar

1 teaspoon vanilla extract

2 large eggs

1 teaspoon white vinegar

1 tablespoon red food coloring

1/2 cup all-purpose flour

1/3 cup cocoa powder

1/4 teaspoon baking powder

1/4 teaspoon salt

CREAM CHEESE FROSTING

4 ounces cream cheese, softened

1/4 cup (1/2 stick) butter, softened

1 1/2 cups powdered sugar

1/2 cup chopped pecans

For the brownies, preheat the oven to 350 degrees, and spray an 8-inch square baking dish with nonstick spray.

In a medium bowl whisk together the oil, white sugar, vanilla, eggs, vinegar, and food coloring. In another medium bowl whisk together the flour, cocoa, baking powder, and salt. Stir the flour mixture into the egg mixture until well combined. Pour the batter into the baking dish, and bake for 28 to 30 minutes, until a wooden pick inserted near the center comes out clean. Let the brownies cool completely.

For the frosting, combine the cream cheese and butter in a large bowl. Using an electric mixer on medium speed, beat the cream cheese and butter until creamy. Slowly add the powdered sugar, and beat until the frosting is smooth. Spread the frosting evenly on top of the cooled brownies. Sprinkle the pecans over the top, and then cut the brownies into squares. Refrigerate the brownies if you are not serving them shortly after baking.

MAKES 12 SERVINGS.

GRILLED POUND CAKE WITH CHAMPAGNE BERRIES

This is a down-home dessert with a sophisticated twist. Slathering pound cake with butter and grilling it might be the only thing you could ever do to make pound cake better. Feel free to mix up the berries in this recipe with whatever looks the freshest.

8 ounces raspberries

8 ounces blackberries

4 tablespoons sugar, divided

1 cup champagne

1 cup heavy cream

1 (16-ounce) loaf pound cake

1/4 cup (1/2 stick) butter, melted

Place the raspberries and blackberries in a medium bowl, and toss them with 2 tablespoons of the sugar. Pour the champagne over the berries, and refrigerate for 30 minutes.

Place the cream in a large bowl. Using an electric mixer, beat the cream on medium speed until soft peaks form. Add the remaining 2 tablespoons sugar, and continue beating just until the sugar is mixed in. Refrigerate the whipped cream until you are ready to serve it.

Slice the pound cake into 1-inch slices. Heat the grill to medium-high heat. Brush the cake slices with the melted butter, and grill the slices for about 2 minutes per side, until grill marks are formed. Remove the slices from the grill, and top each cake slice with the berries and whipped cream.

MAKES 6 TO 8 SERVINGS.

Old-Fashioned Cherry Hand Pies

I prefer to use frozen, pitted cherries for these adorable hand pies because who really wants to pit cherries? I also cut down on time by using a prepared piecrust so these really do come together quickly. The maraschino cherries are my secret ingredient in these pies; they are deliciously sweet and chewy.

2 cups frozen pitted cherries, chopped (they do not need to be thawed)

1/4 cup maraschino cherries, drained and chopped

1 tablespoon fresh lemon juice

3 tablespoons brown sugar

2 tablespoons cornstarch

1/4 teaspoon salt

1/4 teaspoon almond extract

2 refrigerated 9-inch piecrusts

1 large egg, beaten

2 tablespoons raw or turbinado sugar

In a medium bowl toss together the chopped cherries, maraschino cherries, lemon juice, brown sugar, cornstarch, salt, and almond extract.

Preheat the oven to 375 degrees. Roll the pie dough out to 10 inches in diameter, and cut 5-inch diameter circles out of the dough; you should get 8 circles from the two piecrusts. Place the dough circles on two baking sheets. Use a slotted spoon to put a little of the cherry mixture into the center of each dough circle, being careful not to overstuff them. Fold the dough over the filling to form a semicircle, and seal the edges well by pressing with a fork. Continue until all of the pies are made. Brush the pies with the beaten egg, and sprinkle them evenly with the raw sugar. Bake the pies for 20 to 25 minutes, until they are golden brown. Let the pies cool slightly before serving them with vanilla ice cream.

MAKES 8 SERVINGS.

"Spring Is in the Air" Coconut Cupcakes

There is just something about these cupcakes that screams springtime, my favorite time of the year. I love the light and fluffy texture with the sweet crunch of the toasted coconut. It's almost impossible to have just one.

Coconut Cupcakes

1 (15-ounce) box white cake mix

1 (13 1/2 -ounce) can coconut milk

4 large egg whites

1/3 cup canola oil

Coconut Frosting

1 cup (2 sticks) butter, softened

4 cups powdered sugar

1/4 cup heavy cream

1/2 teaspoon vanilla extract

1 1/2 cups flaked, sweetened coconut

For the cupcakes, preheat the oven to 350 degrees. Line two 12-count muffin tins with 22 cupcake liners.

Place the cake mix, coconut milk, egg whites, and oil in a large bowl. Using a mixer on medium speed, beat the ingredients for about 2 minutes. Fill the cupcake liners three-fourths full with the batter. Bake the cupcakes for 18 to 20 minutes, and then let them cool completely on a wire rack.

For the frosting, place the butter in a large bowl. Using the electric mixer on medium speed, beat the butter until creamy. Gradually add the powdered sugar, beating until the mixture is smooth. Next add the cream and vanilla, and continue beating the frosting until it is light and fluffy.

Spread the flaked coconut onto a baking sheet, and toast it for 2 to 3 minutes in the 350-degree oven. Stir the coconut around, and bake it for another 2 to 3 minutes, until most of the coconut is golden brown.

Spread the frosting on the cooled cupcakes, and then dip the tops of the cakes into the toasted coconut.

Makes 22 servings.

Fourth of July Mason Jar Trifles

My mom used to make a cake for the 4th of July that had strawberries and blueberries; you have probably seen the one I'm talking about. It was always the perfect ending to a day of grilling out with family and friends. These adorable Mason jar trifles are my riff on that light, festive cake from my childhood.

2 (2-ounce) packages instant vanilla pudding

4 cups milk

1 pound strawberries, sliced

2 pints blueberries

2 tablespoons fresh lemon juice

2 tablespoons sugar

Prepared angel food cake, cut into small cubes

6 Mason jars

Extra strawberries and/or blueberries to garnish

In a large bowl whisk together the instant pudding and the milk until the pudding has thickened. Refrigerate until you are ready to assemble the trifles. Place the strawberries and blueberries in a large bowl, and toss with the lemon juice and sugar. Allow the berries to sit for at least 10 minutes to macerate.

Once you are ready to assemble the trifles, spoon some of the pudding into each jar, then add a layer of the cake pieces, and top the cake layer with the berries and their juices. Continue these layers once more, and top with a final layer of pudding. Add a sliced strawberry or fresh blueberries on top to garnish, if desired. Cover the trifles with the jar lids, and chill until you are ready to serve.

MAKES 6 SERVINGS.

MA'S RAISIN PIE

This raisin pie has been handed down to me from my great-grandmother Ma. I happen to love raisins; put them in a pie and serve a scoop of vanilla ice cream, and I'm a happy a girl!

1 (9-inch) refrigerated piecrust

2 1/2 cups raisins

2 1/4 cups water

2/3 cup firmly packed brown sugar

2 tablespoons cornstarch

1 teaspoon finely grated orange peel

1 teaspoon ground cinnamon

1/4 teaspoon salt

1 tablespoon white vinegar

2 tablespoons butter

Preheat the oven to 400 degrees. Line a 9-inch pie plate with the piecrust, and set it aside. Place the raisins and water in a saucepan over high heat. Bring to a boil, cook for 5 minutes, and then remove from heat.

In a large bowl mix together the brown sugar, cornstarch, orange peel, cinnamon, and salt. Stir the raisins into the sugar mixture. Stir in the vinegar and butter until the butter is

melted and the mixture has slightly thickened. Pour the filling into the crust, and bake the pie for 35 to 40 minutes. Let the pie cool for at least 1 hour before slicing.

MAKES 8 SERVINGS.

TOFFEE PECAN SANDIES

Pecan sandies were one of those cookies we always had in the pantry growing up, although I didn't totally appreciate them until I became an adult. Now I fully understand why my family loved the buttery goodness in these crumbly, nutty cookies.

---

1 cup (2 sticks) butter, softened

1/2 cup firmly packed brown sugar

2 cups all-purpose flour

3/4 teaspoon salt

1/2 cup finely chopped pecans

1/2 cup toffee bits

Cooking spray

Place the butter and sugar in a large bowl. Using an electric mixer on medium speed, beat the mixture until creamy. Mix in the flour and salt, and then add in the pecans and toffee until everything is thoroughly combined. Wrap the dough in plastic wrap, and refrigerate it for at least 30 minutes.

Preheat the oven to 325 degrees. Spray a baking sheet with cooking spray. Pinch off 1 1/2-inch pieces of the dough, and roll them into balls. Place on the baking sheet, 1 inch apart. Gently press the balls with the bottom of a glass. Bake the cookies for 12 minutes. Transfer them to a wire rack to cool completely.

MAKES 24 COOKIES.

BANANA CREAM WHOOPIE PIES

Bell Buckle, Tennessee, not far from my hometown of Murfreesboro, is the home of Moon Pies. I grew up on these marshmallow-filled cookie sandwiches, and this banana version takes me right back to the good old days. Moon Pies are similar to the gourmet whoopie pies that are so popular nowadays, and this recipe is a cross between the two.

COOKIES

1/2 cup (1 stick) butter, softened

1 cup white sugar

1 teaspoon vanilla extract

1 large egg

2 cups all-purpose flour

1/2 teaspoon baking soda

1/2 teaspoon baking powder

3/4 teaspoon salt

1/2 cup sour cream

1 cup mashed ripe banana

CREAM FILLING

1/2 cup (1 stick) butter, softened

1 (7-ounce) jar marshmallow cream

1 1/2 cups powdered sugar

For the cookies, preheat the oven to 350 degrees. Grease a baking sheet. Place the butter and white sugar in a large bowl. Using an electric mixer on medium speed, beat the butter and sugar until light and fluffy. Mix in the vanilla and egg until they are well combined. In a medium bowl whisk together the flour, baking soda, baking powder, and salt. In a small bowl mix together the sour cream and mashed banana. Add the flour mixture and the banana mixture alternately to the butter mixture, beating until everything is well combined. Drop the batter by heaping tablespoonsful onto the baking sheet 2 inches apart. Bake the cookies for 12 to 14 minutes.

Transfer the cookies to a wire rack, and let them cool completely.

For the filling, place the butter and marshmallow cream in a large bowl. Using the electric mixer, beat them until well combined. Slowly mix in the powdered sugar until the filling is smooth. Place a tablespoon of the filling onto half of the cookies, and then top them with the remaining cookies to make 12 whoopie pies. Wrap each pie in plastic wrap for easy transporting.

MAKES 12 SERVINGS.

SUNFLOWER CONCERT SERIES

STATE BOTANICAL GARDEN OF GEORGIA
ATHENS, GEORGIA
JUNE THROUGH SEPTEMBER
WWW.BOTGARDEN.UGA.EDU

While Athens, Georgia, is primarily known as the home of the Georgia Bulldogs, this eclectic college town is also home to the 313-acre State Botanical Garden of Georgia. This is one of Athens's most visited attractions as well as a beautiful venue for summer concerts. The Sunflower Concert Series includes four concerts held in the evenings from June through September on the stage of the terraced Flower Garden.

Attendees are encouraged to get cozy, bring a picnic dinner and a blanket, and enjoy a variety of local music. Since there is so much to see at this breathtaking setting, it's a good idea to come early in order to explore all that the gardens have to offer. The concerts get started at 7:00 pm, which gives you plenty of time to admire the surroundings and work up an appetite for a relaxed, family-friendly evening at the garden.

Peachy Biscuit Bread Pudding with Warm Whiskey Sauce

Peaches and biscuits are two of my most favorite things! This pudding is one of those desserts that you are guaranteed not to have any leftovers, even if you only have four people eating it. This one really has the best of all things Southern put together for one irresistible bread pudding.

Bread Pudding

6 to 8 biscuits, baked and crumbled (about 5 cups)

2 cups peeled and sliced pitted peaches

1/2 cup chopped pecans

1 1/2 cups half-and-half

2 large eggs

1/2 cup firmly packed brown sugar

1 teaspoon vanilla extract

1/2 teaspoon salt

Whiskey Sauce

1/4 cup half-and-half

1/2 cup firmly packed brown sugar

2 tablespoons whiskey

1/4 teaspoon salt

1/4 cup (1/2 stick) butter

For the pudding, preheat the oven to 350 degrees. Combine the biscuits, peaches, and pecans in a large bowl, and then place them in a 9-inch square baking dish. Whisk together the half-and-half, eggs, brown sugar, vanilla, and salt in a large bowl. Pour the cream mixture over the biscuit mixture, and let it sit for 10 minutes. Bake the bread pudding for 40 minutes, or until it is set, and then let it cool for 10 minutes.

For the sauce, whisk together the half-and-half, brown sugar, whiskey, salt, and butter in a small saucepan over medium-low heat. Cook, stirring frequently, until it is smooth and creamy, for 4 to 5 minutes. Remove the pan from the heat, and serve the sauce over the warm bread pudding.

Makes 6 to 8 servings.

Salted Caramel and Pecan Ice Cream

This ice cream takes a little time, but each component of it is so delicious that it is worth every minute. Making caramel can be a little intimidating, but once you try it a few times, it really is pretty simple. Toasting the pecans is also an essential step in this recipe to get the most flavor and the perfect crunch in every bite.

Caramel

1 cup sugar

$1/4$ cup ($1/2$ stick) butter, softened and cut into 4 pieces

$1/2$ cup heavy cream

2 teaspoons sea salt

Ice Cream

$3/4$ cup sugar

6 large eggs

2 $1/4$ cups half-and-half

1 teaspoon vanilla extract

$1/2$ cup chopped pecans

For the caramel, place the sugar in a heavy saucepan over medium heat, and whisk it until it begins to melt. Stop whisking once the sugar has melted, and wait until it becomes a dark amber color or reaches 350 degrees on a candy thermometer. Immediately remove the pan from the heat, and stir in the butter until it melts. Then slowly stir in the cream and salt. Let the caramel cool to room temperature, and then refrigerate until you are ready to use it.

For the ice cream, in a large glass bowl whisk together the sugar and egg yolks until pale yellow and light in texture. Pour the half-and-half into a medium saucepan, and cook over medium heat until it begins to foam on the edges. Remove the saucepan from the heat, and slowly pour the hot half-and-half into the egg yolk mixture while constantly whisking.

Place the glass bowl over a saucepan with 2 inches of simmering water. Continue to cook and stir until the custard thickens and coats the back of the spoon, for 12 to 15 minutes. Remove the bowl from the saucepan, add the vanilla, and let the custard cool to room temperature. Cover the custard with plastic wrap, allowing the wrap to touch the surface of the custard to keep a film from forming. Refrigerate the custard until it's completely chilled. Pour the custard into a 1 1/2-quart ice-cream freezer, and freeze it according to the manufacturer's directions.

While the ice cream is churning, place the pecans in a dry skillet over medium heat, and cook, tossing them occasionally, until they are toasted, for 8 to 10 minutes. Let them cool completely. Add the pecans to the ice cream for the last minute of churning.

Place one-third of the ice cream in a

freezer-safe container. Spoon about half of the caramel sauce over the top. Repeat these layers, and then place the remaining ice cream over the top. Place the ice cream in the freezer for 2 to 3 hours before serving.

MAKES 6 SERVINGS.

TIP: This recipe makes more than enough caramel sauce for the ice cream, so if you have some leftover, just store it in the refrigerator in an airtight container for up to 2 weeks.

CHUNKY MONKEY FUDGE POPS

Rich fudgy popsicles were a childhood favorite of mine, especially during the warmer months. I decided to recreate them by kicking up the flavor and texture in these frozen treats with some bananas and peanut butter, a classic combination.

1/2 cup sugar

1/4 cup cocoa powder

3 tablespoons cornstarch

1/4 teaspoon salt

2 cups low-fat or whole milk

1/4 cup chunky peanut butter

1/3 cup semisweet chocolate chips

1 medium banana, lightly mashed

6 (3- or 4-ounce) popsicle molds

In a medium saucepan whisk together the sugar, cocoa powder, cornstarch, and salt. Slowly whisk in the milk, and place the saucepan over medium heat. Bring the mixture to a low boil, and cook for 1 minute, stirring constantly. Remove the pan from the heat, and stir in the peanut butter and chocolate chips until they melt into the pudding. Let the pudding cool to room temperature, and then stir in the banana until it is mixed throughout.

Pour the mixture into the popsicle molds.

Insert the sticks in the center of each one, and freeze the popsicles for at least 4 hours.

MAKES 6 SERVINGS.

TIP: Once the popsicles have frozen, run a little warm water over the molds to help loosen them from the molds.

Bourbon Chocolate Bundt Cake

This moist Bundt cake packs a serious bourbon punch. It's topped off with a sweet butter pecan glaze that is the perfect complement to the rich chocolate and bourbon flavor of the cake.

Cake

1/2 cup semisweet chocolate chips

3/4 cup (1 1/2 stick) butter

1 1/2 cups white sugar

1 teaspoon vanilla extract

1 large egg

2 cups all-purpose flour

1/2 cup cocoa powder

1 tablespoon baking soda

3/4 teaspoon salt

1/2 teaspoon ground cinnamon

1 cup sour cream

1/2 cup bourbon

1/2 cup water

Butter Pecan Glaze

1/4 cup (1/2 stick) butter

1/3 cup chopped pecans

3/4 cup firmly packed brown sugar

1/4 teaspoon salt

1/4 cup heavy cream

For the cake, preheat the oven to 350 degrees, and butter and dust a Bundt pan with cocoa powder. Place a large glass bowl over a saucepan of shallow simmering water. Add the chocolate chips and butter to the bowl, and stir them together until they are completely melted. Remove the bowl from the heat, let the mixture cool slightly, and then whisk in the white sugar, vanilla, and egg.

In a medium bowl whisk together the flour, cocoa powder, baking soda, salt, and cinnamon. Add one-third of the flour mixture to the chocolate mixture, and then stir in the sour cream. Add another one-third of the flour mixture, and then stir in the bourbon and water. Stir in the remaining flour mixture. Pour the batter into the Bundt pan, and bake the cake for 40 to 45 minutes, until a wooden pick inserted near the center comes out clean. Let the cake cool for at least 45 minutes before removing it from the pan.

For the glaze, melt the butter in a medium saucepan over medium heat. Add the pecans, and then stir in the brown sugar and salt. Cook for 2 minutes. Stir in the heavy cream, cooking and stirring for another 2 minutes. Remove the pan from the heat, and let the glaze cool to room temperature. Pour the glaze over the cooled cake, allowing it to drizzle down the sides.

Makes 10 to 12 servings.

Ukulele Picnic in Hawaii

KAKA'AKO WATERFRONT PARK
Honolulu, Hawaii
Dates Vary. Check website for specific details
Ukulelepicnicinhawaii.org

The annual Ukulele Picnic in Honolulu honors Hawaii's favorite instrument. It includes a fund-raising concert, an international ukulele contest, a hula show, and the picnic itself. The best professionals as well as amateurs in the world gather each year to show off their talents in a show that could only take place in Hawaii.

Players from Hawaii, Japan, and elsewhere make music along Oahu's south shore during the picnic from the morning until sunset. The free festival at Kakaako Waterfront Park features a variety of booths containing Hawaiian crafts and food and offering activities for kids.

Celebrating the gift of the ukulele with the world, this festival is a perfect place to kick back and enjoy a good meal as well as the aloha spirit.

MONIE'S SHASTA CAKE

When my mother and her three sisters were growing up, their mother would make this cake in the mornings for potlucks at the bank where she worked. All of the girls would smell it baking as they were getting ready for school knowing they couldn't have any, which was just miserable, I'm sure! This cake recipe will be passed on for generations in my family because it's always such a huge hit anywhere you take it.

CAKE

Cooking spray

$^1/_2$ cup (1 stick) butter

$^1/_2$ cup canola oil

1 cup water

2 large eggs

$^1/_2$ cup sour cream

1 teaspoon vanilla extract

2 cups self-rising flour

1 $^1/_2$ cups white sugar

2 tablespoons cocoa powder

1 teaspoon ground cinnamon

1 teaspoon baking soda

FROSTING

$^1/_2$ cup (1 stick) butter, softened

1 teaspoon vanilla extract

$^1/_4$ cup cocoa powder

2 $^1/_4$ cups powdered sugar

$^1/_4$ cup whole or low-fat milk

$^1/_2$ cup chopped walnuts

For the cake, preheat the oven to 375 degrees, and spray a 13 x 9-inch baking dish with cooking spray. Combine the butter, oil, and water in a small saucepan, and bring to a boil over medium-high heat. Let cool. In a large bowl mix together the eggs, sour cream, and vanilla. In a medium bowl whisk together the self-rising flour, white sugar, cocoa powder, cinnamon, and baking soda. Mix the flour mixture into the egg mixture, and then stir in the cooled butter mixture. Pour the batter into the prepared dish, and bake the cake for 30 minutes.

For the frosting, place the butter, vanilla, and cocoa powder in a large bowl, and using an electric mixer on medium speed, beat until smooth. Gradually mix in the powdered sugar and the milk until the frosting is smooth. Fold in the walnuts.

Let the cake cool for about 5 minutes, and then gently spread the frosting over the warm cake. Let the cake cool completely before slicing and serving it.

MAKES 12 TO 16 SERVINGS.

ACKNOWLEDGMENTS

Writing this cookbook has been an absolute dream come true for me! Getting pregnant in the middle of writing it was certainly not in my plans, but with the help of some very special people we pulled it off, and I could not be more thrilled with the outcome.

Bryan Curtis took a chance on me and believed in my ability as a recipe creator enough to guide me through writing my first cookbook. His vision for the book has been my inspiration throughout the entire creative process. I am so grateful for his help and his confidence in me.

Heather Skelton at Thomas Nelson has not only been a huge help in completing this book, she has also become a dear friend. During the editing of this book we have both had our share of unplanned events including surgeries, a flooded house, and going into labor three weeks early. Through it all, she never skipped a beat and has worked with me in the midst all of the craziness to make this book the best it can be.

Tammy Algood has been my mentor and cheerleader. Her generosity and willingness to offer advice and wisdom about cookbook writing, television segments, and life in general mean more than she will ever know.

Stephanie Mullins and Teresa Blackburn have been an absolute joy to work with! I was just giddy during the photo shoots as I watched these talented ladies turn my recipes into beautiful art.

My parents have always encouraged me to follow my heart and do what I love. Their support and unconditional love have been some of the greatest gifts in my life.

My husband, Zach, has been my taste tester, my last-minute grocery runner, and my teammate. Over the past four years, he has sacrificed so much so that I could keep pursuing my dreams. I am beyond thankful for my very best friend and father to our sweet son.

THE LORD HAS DONE GREAT THINGS FOR US, AND WE ARE FILLED WITH JOY.
—PSALM 126:3

About the Author

April McKinney is an award-winning cook, food writer, and recipe demonstrator from Franklin, Tennessee. April's ease in front of the camera and talent in the kitchen have resulted in her winning several national recipe video contests, giving her the opportunity to cook with popular Food Network stars. Her contest winnings have also given her opportunities to demonstrate her recipes on national TV shows including the *TODAY* show and *BetterTV*.

April has combined her love of performing and cooking to create her own YouTube channel and recipe website. She can also be seen on *Talk of the Town* in Nashville, demonstrating her newest recipes. She encourages people to create healthy, simple, and delicious meals while having fun in the kitchen. Her recipe inspirations come from her Southern upbringing and her love of farm-fresh ingredients.

INDEX

DESTINATION INDEX

NOTE: In this cookbook, the grilling recipes are written for a gas grill. If you prefer to use a charcoal grill, light the charcoal, and then spread it to build your fire. If you are cooking over high heat, light enough charcoal to have a double layer; for lower heat, use only a single layer of charcoal. For indirect heat, push all of the charcoal to one side of the coal grate and cook on the other side of the grill.

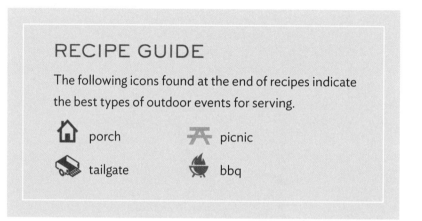

RECIPE GUIDE

The following icons found at the end of recipes indicate the best types of outdoor events for serving.

porch   picnic

tailgate   bbq

INTRODUCTION

I have developed such a deep appreciation for the tradition of gathering around an outdoor table. In fact, my most vivid memories from my childhood are of the many backyard barbecues that included my grandpa's chicken wings and my mom's frosted brownies. My cousins and I spent many summer days with a picnic lunch in my grandmother's garden. Afternoons by the pool were for sipping fresh lemonade and digging into ruby-red watermelon with a sprinkle of salt.

As a young married couple, my husband and I have already established a love of eating outdoors, whether it's just the two of us or with the people we love. As we begin our own family, my wish is that my children will also spend many summer evenings outdoors, nibbling on appetizers and sides in between catching fireflies, with the sound of adult laughter in the background. These are the sweet memories of my childhood, and I can't wait for my little ones to experience the same carefree days and nights under the stars.

As much as my family, friends, and I love entertaining on porches and patios, we also love packing up a picnic basket or cooler for a night of entertainment or a day of tailgating. So along with all kinds of amazing recipes in this book, I have included a variety of special events and outdoor venues that will give you the perfect opportunity to try out some of these tasty dishes. From the early spring to late in the fall, there are outdoor venues where you can enjoy live music, dancing, movies, and tailgating, of course! Be sure to check the websites for these events as dates and times can change each year.

In an age of televisions, computers, and technology, eating outdoors gives us the rare opportunity to simply be entertained by good food and great company. My hope is that as you flip through the pages of this book, you will be excited by these recipes enough to host a "just because" barbecue or pack up a picnic and make some priceless memories with the ones you love. May this book be the inspiration behind many sweet days filled with warm sunshine, heavenly food, and lots of laughter.

CONTENTS

Published in Nashville, Tennessee, by Nelson Books, an imprint of Thomas Nelson. Nelson Books and Thomas Nelson are registered trademarks of HarperCollins Christian Publishing, Inc.

Scripture quotations are taken from The Holy Bible, New International Version®, NIV® Copyright © 1973, 1978, 1984, 2011 by Biblica, Inc.® Used by permission. All rights reserved worldwide.

Photography by Stephanie Mullins

Food and Prop Styling by Teresa Blackburn

Thomas Nelson, Inc., titles may be purchased in bulk for educational, business, fund-raising, or sales promotional use. For information, please e-mail SpecialMarkets@ThomasNelson.com.

Library of Congress Control Number: 2015930052

ISBN-13: 978-0-7180-2219-8

Printed in the United States of America

15 16 17 18 19 QG 6 5 4 3 2 1

THE
OUTDOOR
TABLE

THE ULTIMATE COOKBOOK FOR YOUR NEXT BACKYARD BBQ, FRONT-PORCH MEAL, TAILGATE, OR PICNIC

APRIL MCKINNEY

NELSON
BOOKS

An Imprint of Thomas Nelson